T0156411

INTO THE
NEW MILLENNIUM

NEW JERSEY AND THE NATION

HALL INSTITUTE OF PUBLIC POLICY
– NEW JERSEY

iUniverse, Inc.
Bloomington

Into the New Millennium
New Jersey and the Nation

iUniverse books may be ordered through booksellers or by contacting:

iUniverse
1663 Liberty Drive
Bloomington, IN 47403
www.iuniverse.com
1-800-Authors (1-800-288-4677)

ISBN: 978-1-4620-1902-1 (sc)
ISBN: 978-1-4620-1903-8 (hc)
ISBN: 978-1-4620-1904-5 (e)

Printed in the United States of America

iUniverse rev. date: 5/27/2011

FOREWORD

The Hall Institute of Public Policy – New Jersey has been intensely involved in examining critical issues that impact on both the state and the nation. Those problems have been associated with the massive economic decline of the last several years—the worse since the Great Depression of the 1930s. The broad sweep of the volume here in some ways mirrors the complexities of the time. This is the fourth volume of essays that the Hall Institute has completed. The first two were printed, and mailed out to opinion makers and major libraries. The third volume was put on our website, as is this one. In the last several years, the Institute has become more multimedia in its presentations, embracing aspects of the newer social media as well, and its effects can be seen on the website HallNJ.org.

There has been increasing concern with our public schools and the desire to create alternatives, including charter schools, a position which is examined by Jarrett E. Chapin, a former staff member of the Institute. The large numbers of teachers projected to retire make that development also a matter of national and state concern.

A comprehensive study of the stock market and the financial crisis offers important lessons to those interested in the public policy aspects of what may be the most important demography shift of our generation, both Dr. Linda Stamato and Gerald P. O'Driscoll Jr. show. In New Jersey, state leaders have been dealing with the increasing gap between assets and liabilities in its pension system. The Hall Institute has compiled one of the most informed examinations on that issue – one that focuses on the need for new management structures and new policies and procedures to govern future investment choices.

Health care has consumed much public attention—including obesity, new strains of flu, and the cleanliness of hospitals. A national and international concern is the growing number of cases of diabetes, and the National Conference of State Legislatures has provided an important overview. On a lighter note, the future of NASA and its great adventures in space exploration has received new scrutiny in this Obama Administration. The costs of manned space flights have so increased that government sponsorship may soon decrease. Some of the romance is over.

An understanding of history is important to New Jerseyans. The abysmal record of the Bush administration in the areas of civil right enforcement has gained more than just cursory interest in a major report presented here. And the U. S. military paints a study that shows how the percentage of deaths and casualties from Al Qaeda attacks affects many more Moslem peoples than Christians.

Lastly, 2009 was the 200th anniversary of the birth of America's greatest president, Abraham Lincoln. Lincoln had little electoral support in New Jersey but, as historian William Gillette has shown, the Jersey Blues troops fought long and valiantly for the Union cause. I am proud to acknowledge that the Hall Institute has been the major sponsor of the New Jersey Abraham Lincoln Bicentennial Commission. One continuing point of controversy has been what was the real cause of the Civil War, and my selection looks at the most obvious cause—the dynamics of human bondage.

In the production of this volume, my sincere thanks to William J. Richards and to Eunice Lee.

— Michael P. Riccards

CONTENTS

Chapter One

Charter School Performance in Sixteen States

By
Jarrett E. Chapin

Study Methodology

Stanford University's Center for Research on Education Outcomes (CREDO) has released new findings about American choice schools in 16 states. The first of three reports scheduled to be released in 2009, "Multiple Choice: Charter School Performance in 16 States" searches for measures of charter school "effectiveness." CREDO chooses student outcomes or standardized test scores as an indicator of effectiveness. Specifically, the approach is a value added approach which takes initial student scores as a base which can be removed from latter scores in order to measure the charter school's effect on score growth.

The data in the report, a project undertaken with the use of a data collection methodology pioneered by RAND Corp., is an advance over previous studies as it utilized standardized data from a good number of charter schools nationally, about "1.7 million records from more than 2400 charter schools." Standard data allows for a reading of charter school characteristics between individual states that are comparable. Also, taken as a whole, the data is representative of all charter schools on the national level. CREDO notes: "the states included in this study enroll more than half the charter school students in the United States, so the consolidated results begin, for the first time, to tell the story of the policy of charter schooling at a macro level."

In order to mitigate the effects of selection bias, the CREDO researchers employ a Virtual Control Record (VCR) methodology by which a virtual twin for each student in the study is created to be sure that both charter students and the traditional public school (TPS) students are comparable. Basically, by taking both charter and TPS students from the same origin, the students are considered characteristically similar. CREDO explains thus:

"We identify all the TPS that have students who transfer to a given charter school; we call each of these schools 'feeder schools.' Once a school qualifies as a feeder school, all the students in the school become potential matches for a student in a particular charter school. All the student records from all the feeder schools are pooled – this becomes the source of records for creating the virtual match. Using the records of the students in those schools in the year prior to the test year of interest, CREDO selects all of the available records that match each charter school student."

Study Findings

To begin, CREDO's major findings do not do much to champion the cause of charter schools. Their reports finds the following: on average, charter students experience a decrease in math and reading when compared to students in traditional public schools. But these aren't the most interesting findings in the report. The most interesting conclusion, in fact, is probably that the students performing best in choice schools happen to be English Language Learners (ELL) and students in poverty. Also, despite there being a significant demographic overlap between students in poverty and many American minority groups, CREDO finds that Black and Hispanic charter school student performance is "significantly worse" when compared to the performance of demographically comparable students (data twins) enrolled in traditional public schools. The two conclusions together are interesting in as much as charter schools are often viewed, specifically, as a positive alternative to TPS education for low income students which, as mentioned, tend to overlap demographically with minority groups. This is troubling information, though the report mentions that the statistics do not yet reveal any specific causes to account for the data.

According to the report, race and economic status are not the only determinants of educational outcomes. Time and education level are also factors. In regard to time, CREDO researchers find:

"Students do better in charter schools over time. First year charter students on average experience a decline in learning, which may reflect a combination of mobility effects and the experience of a charter school in its early years. Second and third years in charter schools see a significant reversal to positive gains."

Regarding education level, charter school students at the elementary and middle school level were found to have learned at "higher rates" than their peers in TPSs and at lower rates on the high school level. From another vantage, a charter that serves only high school level students may be predictably worse. The proper niche for charters, therefore, may be in serving the lower grades, a conclusion that must be considered by policy makers as perhaps now more than 48 percent of all charters, according to Center for Education Reform data in 2005, serve students on the high school level. Further, in regard to CREDO's prior conclusions, the National Charter School Research Project also concluded in 2005 that "nationally, charter schools serve a larger proportion of minority and low-income students than is found in traditional public schools, a characteristic due largely to the disproportionate number of charter schools located in urban areas." Often, the mission of charter school education reform is to offer to minority and underserved communities a positive alternative to their local TPSs which are by many reformers considered to be the root cause of unsatisfactory educational outcomes. This thought, presumably, is what has motivated the CREDO researchers to undertake the comparison. However, CREDO's data may run contrary to the intuitions of many reformers. And, there is a danger that, if policy makers are not informed, certain communities will be harmed by the same act of reform that was intended to serve them and their children better. Indeed, if the data allows us to do so, taking all the report's conclusions together produces the image of the ideal charter: the ideal is a charter that serves only non-Hispanic and non-Black students in grades K-8. Of what use, we might then ask, is such a school?

These questions aside, once they are reproduced and thus confirmed in other studies these conclusions should have a significant impact on the way policy makers view charter schools in their own states. Knowing how and for whom charter schools work best might cause education officials to pause before closing an underperforming school as, for instance, the number of first year students enrolled at a charter may bear significantly on educational outcomes reported for a certain year. In this way, for officials, the "first year effect" might be actively treated with some new policy, or acknowledged as more an enrollment phenomenon rather than a determinant of charter failure. Rather than contributing to keeping charters open, however, researchers understand that their efforts may have the opposite effect as keeping charters open is not the greatest challenge facing charter school reform, currently in an "authorizing crisis." CREDO describes that "Evidence of financial insolvency or corrupt governance structure, less easy to dispute or defend, is much more likely to lead to school closures than poor academic performance." As poor performing schools do more harm than good to the charter reform movement by corrupting the data gleaned from successful charters, from the perspective of statistical research, CREDO suggests that their work should add imperative to the difficult task of closing underperforming schools. Unfortunately, according to their research, many of these underperforming schools may serve the majority of at risk students.

Policy Environment

Perhaps more interesting than the forgoing conclusions, the effect of policy environment on charter school effectiveness will be particularly useful to officials and those who study governance and education administration. Studying the following: "the use of a cap on the supply of charters"; "the availability of multiple authorizers"; and "the availability of an appeals process to review authorizer decisions." Caps, presumably, limit the total number or charters and thus the overall number of low performing charters by increasing the pressure to close old and to grant entry to new charters. More authorizers may add more knowledge to support judgments about closing or authorization—and it may also permit poor performing schools to pick sympathetic judges. Lastly, the opportunity to appeal the decision of an authorizer may "increase the proportion of marginal schools, dragging down the overall performance of the sector" or it may add a higher level of scrutiny to authorizer judgments, the CREDO researchers suggest. Briefly, CREDO found that the existence of charter caps lowers student performance in a state; multiple authorizers has "a significant negative impact on student academic growth"; the opportunity for appeal seemed to have a growth effect for student academic outcomes, though the conclusions are tentative because none of the states changed their policies during the study period.

In the report, there is also included the breakdown into math and reading performance for several kinds of students and the analysis of outcomes with both charter and TPS understood in a market framework. At large, much of the research really draws attention to how subtle the differences are between charter and TPS environments. The subtlety of the differences almost lends support to less recent studies that conclude no significant difference between charter and TPS. However, though these differences are subtle, they are still important given the size and demography of the student population enrolled in charter schools.

Is it the case that the perfect charter school student looks something like this: in grades K-8, in poverty, an ELL of non-Hispanic or non-Black heritage. Similarly, is the ideal school one which operates in states that: shun caps, have a single authorizing entity and favors appeals? Perhaps these characteristics are only determinants of success when they are each by themselves. By lumping them together we supposes that all these factors are inclusive. Further, making up ideal schools and districts based on the data is interesting but not very productive. If this kind of idealization accomplishes anything it begs us to investigate more - into the why and the how of the CREDO's findings.

New Jersey

Though New Jersey is not part of the CREDO's analysis, a simple inventory of the identified indicators would be interesting. Unfortunately, no data exists for some of the indicators such as race and at-risk which might be why New Jersey was not included among the other states in the charter school study. We do have some information, however. According to the New Jersey Department of Education, over 18,000 New Jersey students attended 62 charter schools as of May 2009. About 13 of those 62 charters serve over 4,413 students, roughly 24.5 percent of all students. Further, regarding state policy, New Jersey, joined by 14 other states, Arizona, Colorado, Delaware, Florida, Georgia, Kansas, Maryland, Minnesota, Nevada, Oregon, Pennsylvania, South Carolina, Virginia, and Wyoming, has no charter school cap. However, the rigorous process of application and accountability to the state's sole authorizer adds a significant amount of a barrier to charter school entry.

Though there is no cap and no leveraged pressure to eliminate low performers, school performance assessment is administered every two years. Upon entry, charters are all granted a four year term, at the end of which they must apply for renewal to the education commissioner.

New Jersey is the only state to invest in one person, the commissioner of education, the responsibility of authorization. As most other states charge single or multiple boards with that responsibility, the effects of New Jersey's unique charter policy and that of other states are not comparable in studies such as the foregoing.

New Jersey's appeal process is open to the affected school district as well as the charter operator as a means of reconsidering an authorizer's decision. Appeals are directed to the State Board of Education. Whether this has an effect on growth in New Jersey charters is uncertain. By 2005, New Jersey had authorized 91 charter school applications and had received 237 in total. Despite the availability of appeal, the number of charters in New Jersey has never grown over 67, the number reached in 2005. No great augmentation of the charter school count has occurred since the beginning of charter schools in New Jersey.

Though the performance of New Jersey's charters cannot be directly understood in reference to the CREDO findings, it would still be interesting to add to this study the relative effects that New Jersey's policy environment has on student performance. Policy makers should pay attention to this and the following two reports from CREDO as, even if they do not support them as a solution to the education of underserved student populations, there is much to be learned about the education environment of traditional public schools in the laboratory environment of the charters.

Chapter Two

History and Future of New Jersey Pensions

The Hall Institute of Public Policy – New Jersey[1]

Executive Summary

The current full liability of the New Jersey pension fund is estimated to be approximately $118 billion of which $28 billion is unfunded (2007). In order to make up this gap, either higher contributions from state employees and/ or the state government, or very significant investment returns are needed. After significant review and research, we believe that the management structures that once served the system need to be seriously re-examined by the Legislature and the Governor. Currently the State Investment Council, which mainly deals with investment policy, is composed of unpaid individuals with significant experience in asset management who give of their time and effort. The state is fortunate in being able to attract such people. Now, however, the extreme volatility of the market, the difficulties being faced by non-American markets, the loss of major players in the financial industry, and the much more intrusive role of the government in the market all have led to an environment we have not seen before. The pension fund has absorbed substantial losses, and the media now is paying significant attention to stories such as the state's failed investment in Lehman Brothers and its increased allocation to a BlackRock fund to stave off forced liquidations. We believe these issues need to be studied and dealt with dispassionately.

It is our view that the investment process undertaken by the Fund

---

1   Research for this report on the history of the New Jersey pension system and all personal interviews were conducted by Michael P. Riccards, Executive Director of The Hall Institute of Public Policy.

management must be made still more transparent. Conflicts need to be avoided. The responsibilities of the Director of the Division of Investments, the staff, consultants and the State Investment Council need to be more clearly defined. The state needs to invest more in upgrading the investment resources available to the director while creating a new tier of trained and experienced asset managers. We believe that there should be an allocation of assets to outside managers who have skills or niches outside of what state government can achieve internally. We also believe that there must be a genuine recognition of what various levels of investment risk can achieve over the long run, and how that influences levels of benefits and contributions. Finally, we believe that there needs to be a clear recognition that the long-run perspective for investment returns is far longer than that of any gubernatorial administration, and that adjustments to contributions based on swings in markets, positive or negative, must be avoided.

The Investment Council relies heavily on a staff of dedicated professionals who are responsible for enormous investments in the portfolio. As in many public systems, the compensation for staff members is low considering the vast scope of their responsibilities.[2] It is not desirable that these managers be restricted by the state employment system; rather they should have expectations and rewards that are more in line with other public investment agencies and private endowments. The state should examine an enhanced compensation package for the staff. Employment policies should be amended to pay for – and value – ongoing professional training.[3] The staff also needs help. It needs greater depth in its personnel ranks to analyze and perform due diligence on the ever changing criteria involved in investment policy.

Lastly, the major unions who have so much at stake in the process and in the general solvency of the state government should be more willing to support the prudent and flexible use of outside asset managers by the State Investment Council and the staff.[4] The selection of managers should be given great care, free of conflict and very transparent. It should also fit into a well defined and coordinated asset allocation process. There will be higher costs in managing this portfolio than in the past — but in the end these investments are critical to the state's future.

We believe that in the wake of the losses experienced in the pension system recently, the state must re-examine the system, a process that has begun with the Senate Budget and Appropriation Committee's meeting on November 24, 2008. The recommendations in this report are meant to focus positively on steps to be taken.

---

2   Personal interview A.
3   Personal interview C.
4   Personal interview D.

This report will focus on some background as well as the investment process, which is coming under such scrutiny today. For previous Hall Institute articles on the topic of New Jersey's state pensions, visit our website at www.hallnj.org. We welcome other input, and future Hall Institute studies on the pension issue will be forthcoming.

History

Prior to the string of collapses on Wall Street at the end of the summer of 2008, the State of New Jersey was still slowly recovering from a $20 billion depreciation in the pension fund from between 2000 and 2003, when the market value of the pension fund fell from $85.9 billion to $64.2 billion.[5] By the end of 2007, the pension fund was back up to $86.5 billion. As of mid-November of this year, the market value of New Jersey's assets was estimated at $61 billion. The recent and ongoing perils of financial markets and the overall economy have devastated New Jersey. Unfortunately, the damage has been done, and the only thing to do now is to re-evaluate the manner in which the assets are managed going forward and how that relates to the future liabilities and contributions. The bright side is that this time of economic disaster has provided many new opportunities where excess return can be generated with less risk. It is up to the Investment Council and all stakeholders to work together to achieve this goal.

The root of the current problems is not across the river in New York, but rather can be traced back to before 2000 and the Pension Revaluation Act (L.1992, C.41), which was enacted by the state in 1992. Critics charge that, faced with a challenge during the recession of the early 1990s, Governor James Florio contributed to the situation when he applied a speculative innovation to the New Jersey pension system. The purpose of the Pension Revaluation Act of 1992 was to raise money to balance the FY 1993 budget and pay off unfunded cost-of-living adjustments applied to New Jersey pensions in the 1970s.[6] By supplanting the market value (8.75 percent interest rate assumption) for the book value (7 percent interest rate assumption) of pensions, the Florio Administration was able to recalculate $769 million to be applied

---

5   State of New Jersey Benefits Review Task Force "Report of the…" December 1, 2005. P.10.

6   Most notable among the reforms was probably the 1974 Social Security Act amendment, which made cost-of-living (COLA) adjustments mandatory and tied them to the U.S. Bureau of Labor's Consumer Price Index. Albert E. Schwenk, "Compensation in the 1970s" U.S. Bureau of Labor Statistics.

to that end.[7] This strategy of revaluing pensions to market values is now known to have at least one major drawback: it lowered overall state and local contributions to the pension fund. In addition, using the enhanced market value can be problematic in as much as "the valuation at a moment in time can diverge substantially from the price the asset will command when it will be needed to meet pension liabilities."[8] Governor Florio's revaluation served the purpose of balancing the budget and thus indirectly treated the pension as a fiscal buffer. Other programs were not sufficiently cut before pensions were tapped; Governor Florio's innovation proved to be short term, rather than a special strategic or bookkeeping strategy. Critics argue that the policy was questionable and may have paved the way for the series of unfortunate and similar policy decisions that prevailed during the next administration. Governor Florio, however, argues that the movement to market value was actuarially sound, transparent, and similar to what business does.[9]

Having made promises to cut taxes for New Jerseyans during the 1993 campaign, Governor Christine Todd Whitman was forced to seek money in 1994 to try to balance the budget early in her tenure as governor. To this end, Treasurer Brian W. Clymer claimed to have found in the pension fund $1.3 billion extra that been underestimated during the prior administration.[10] Thus, the Pension Reform Act of 1994 (PRA) (L. 1994, C.62),[11] "reduced state and local employer pension contributions to the plan by $547.4 million and $936.8 million for fiscal years 1994 and 1995, respectively."[12] Specifically, the

---

7   Barbara and Stephen Salmore. *New Jersey Politics and Government.* (New Jersey: Rutgers University Press), PP. 209-214.

8   Christian Weller. "Smoothing the Waves of the Perfect Storm". Center for Economic Policy Research.

9   Personal Interview G

10   Ibid. of 7.

11   In Division of Public investment report "Smart Growth Impact":
     (b) A flat five percent pension rate of contribution was enacted by P.L. 1994, [c.62] **c. 62** for all employees enrolled on or after July 1, 1994. For members enrolled prior to July 1, 1994 whose previous full rate of contributions was six percent or more, the five percent contribution rate became effective on July 1, 1995. For members enrolled prior to July 1, 1994 whose previous full rate of contributions was less than six percent, their rate of contributions became four percent on July 1, 1995 and then five percent on July 1, 1996. Effective January 1, 1998 the rate of contribution became four and one half percent. Contributions are currently 5.5 percent.

12   Division of Investment "Disclosure Funding Accounting" April, 2007; At this time, the State not only lowered employer contributions to pension liability but also lowered state aid to employers, which further exacerbated the rising level of unfunded liability.

bill marked a shift in the actuarial funding methodology or the way pension liability is assessed, from the entry age normal (EAN) method to the projected unit credit (PUC). The EAN*[13] allocates the pension based on a standardized percent of the payroll during that period distributing the pension cost over the period between the employee's entry into and retirement from the system.[14] The PUC is overly complex, which may in part be responsible for the problems that would follow the Governor into 1997.

Owing to the shift in assessment methodology, Governor Whitman was, for the moment, able to deliver on her campaign promises to cut taxes, though her great political triumph was soon characterized by some critics as nothing but "smoke and mirrors."[15]

The year 1995 saw American markets achieve dizzying and remarkable increases in wealth. The technology boom of the mid to late 1990s, the so-called "dot-com bubble," was a period of great excitement and of emerging industries and ideas; both were sold at this time with wild abandon and often bought with venture capital.

A year after Governor Whitman's first tax break, the surplus "found" during the assessment methodology shift was really a serious underestimation of New Jersey's pension contribution obligations. The minimum contribution that Governor Whitman had lowered with the PRA caused a situation wherein "the gap between assets and future payments had risen from $800 million in FY 1993 to $4.7 billion in FY 1995; put another way, assets represented only 89 percent of the pension benefit funding level in the latter year, as opposed to 98 percent in the former year."[16] The sudden market enthusiasm and the even more sudden need to set the budget right coalesced into a new bill, the Pension Security Plan (PSP) (L. 1997, C. 115) which issued a bond of $2.75 billion, still "the largest bond issue in history"[17] in order to close the gap between the book value and soaring liability. At the time, the bill was contested by a small coalition of Democrats who filed a lawsuit against the state, insisting that the bond issue should be passed by voters as a referendum. In addition, Moody's Investors Service warned that the increasingly large list of New Jersey's obligations was earning the state a "negative outlook."[18] This

---

13 *EAN is the cost of full benefits for each participant spread as a level amount each year from year of hire to year of retirement. Cost reassigned to fixed period after 10-30 years; PUC is the current actuarial value of a member's future retirement benefits and spread out over years as pensionable income.

14 CalPERS Online Glossary, "Entry Age Normal", Online Oct 1, 2008.

15 Ibid. of 7.

16 Ibid. of 7.

17 Ibid. of 7.

18 Brett Pulley. "Bond Issue In New Jersey Brings In $2.8 Billion." *New York*

made borrowing more difficult and expensive for the state as it increased the perceived likelihood, in the eyes of some lenders, that the state would default.

However, Governor Whitman's plan paid off initially. The market soared during the latter years of the 1990s and the market value of New Jersey pensions, like many other equity-based investments, peaked in 2000 reaching more than $85 billion. This was just before plummeting to $74 billion by June of 2001, and then to just under $66 billion in 2002 when Governor Whitman left the governorship and the pension problem to Acting Governor Donald DiFrancesco. In "Pension Liability vs. Market Value" (Appendix 3), it is clear that had assets been diversified in FY 1999, the state may have had a surplus and New Jersey could have avoided the last few years of fiscal crisis.

The Whitman Administration was able to influence the investment of pensions in the turbulent technology market because at the time most investors were convinced that these assets were sure to pay off for New Jerseyans. It was rational to invest there and therefore prudent to act upon that reason. Said differently, the proposal for a bond issue and the purchase of common stocks, at the time, was credible enough to be considered a prudent investment, though in 1995 there was no actual "prudent investor" criterion in New Jersey law.[19] In New Jersey, the Governor with the consent of the Senate appoints the council members. This process is very different in New York and California. In New York State, there is a sole trustee (comptroller) who is independently elected. In California there is an investment board, an independently elected comptroller and a treasurer. The Governor has some representatives but no control.

Complicating matters, unfunded liability also reached high levels at this time as liability more than doubled from $3.1 billion in 1998 to $7.6 billion in 2000.[20] The PSP in 1997 resulted in either a partial reduction or total elimination "in the State's and local employer's otherwise required normal contributions to the plan for FY 1997 through FY 2003."[21] Also, content enough to supersede contributions and rely heavily on technology driven market growth to finance all pension liabilities, the policies under the Whitman administration made no major efforts to diversify the pension fund's

---

Times, June 26, 1997; Online Sept 28, 2008.

19   Roland M. Machold was nominated to the position of State Treasurer by Gov. Whitman in 1999 after having retired in 1998 from the position of Director of the New Jersey State Division of Investment for 23 years. The nomination from Governor Whitman allowed him to succeed Treasurer James A. DiEleuterio.

20   Ibid of 5.

21   Ibid. of 5.

allocations. In that sense, it joined many in riding the technology boom.
[22] In fact, technology made up about 32 percent of the domestic common
stock allocations in New Jersey in 2000 — about the same percentage as
the overall market capitalization of the U.S. stock market. The question of
course is what should be the real overall allocation to common stocks vs.
other asset classes. The short term market is influenced by booms and busts
that can influence judgments of the pension system. In 2000, New Jersey's
five largest international common stock investments were fairly concentrated
in information technology: Nokia (AB) Oy, Ericsson (Lm) Tel., Alcatel,
Vodafone Group, Nortel Networks Corp. In 2000, IT made up 23 percent
of international allocations. Domestic equity represented 50 percent of the
total portfolio allocations; international, 18 percent.[23]

Some critics argue that it was natural, though not very wise, for the New
Jersey's investment division to have kept the state's funds invested in booming
technology stocks during the late 1990s and early part of the new millennium.
It might have been better, however, to "move into newer asset classes, such as
private equity and real estate" in order to better distribute risk.[24] Ironically,
the lack of investment diversity created a peculiar situation wherein, had
Governor Whitman not halted contributions to pensions at this time, the
damage in 2000 might have been even more severe than was realized. The
state might have then lost not only regular pension assets and the bond of $2.7
billion, but also five years of regular pension contributions to the market.

Aggravating the situation, the state in 2001 granted a broad 9.12 percent
increase in benefits for current and retired state employees just before the
November elections.[25] In tandem with the busting of the dot-com bubble,
this change significantly increased the amount of New Jersey's unfunded
liability. In 2002, state pension contributions were less than 9 percent; in
2006, the state was contributing as much as 16 percent of the budget to
pensions, and assets represented only 79 percent of future liabilities.[26] The
state contributed nothing to the pension funds in 2002 and a minimal amount

22 New Jersey Division of Investment, "Annual Report for Fiscal and Calendar
    Year 2007", June 30, 2007: "New Jersey opted to stay the course and hold
    its asset allocation constant, rather than move into newer asset classes, such
    as private equity and real estate. With the bursting of the "internet bubble"
    in late 2000-2001, the S&P 500 lost 12.8 percent and 16.5 percent for the
    periods from July 1, 2000-June 30, 2001 and July 1, 2001-June 30, 2002,
    respectively."

23 "New Jersey Report for Fiscal year 2000." Investment Section, Division of
    Pensions and Benefits.

24 Ibid. of 7.

25 Ibid. of 7.

26 Ibid. of 7; William Clark Memo, Nov 11, 2008.

in 2006 (pursuant to the 1997 bond sale and the phase-in by the McGreevey Administration).

In FY 2001, New Jersey's returns from pension assets were negative, -10.4 percent; FY 2002 followed suit, -9 percent. New Jersey had been making a slow recovery. The slowness of the recovery is due, in great part, to the decision of Governor James McGreevey's Administration to enact a contribution "phase-in" in FY 2004, L. 2003, c.108. Though the phase-in policy was contributory, and therefore more positive than Governor Whitman's extreme policy of halting contributions all together, this low level of effort continued to increase the state's unfunded accrued liability by pushing off normal contribution levels until 2008.[27] A look at New Jersey's history produces an example of the way the real financial consequences of this marriage of politics and investment are absorbed by taxpayers—a violation of the traditional logic of investment and return. The Manhattan Institute's Nicole Gelinas and E.J. McMahon better articulated this disjunction, calling it an "asymmetry" between politics and investment in a policy brief about a New York bill (A.7597):

Public-sector workers don't take on any investment risk inherent in their own pension fund—taxpayers do. If the [investment manager] invests poorly, taxpayers must pump new cash into the fund, because the constitution guarantees a promised level of benefits to current and future retirees. [...] any potential reward from potentially higher returns will be shared with public-sector workers, in the form of enhanced pension benefits. The dynamic is an object lesson in the perils of fiscal and political asymmetry.[28]

State employees now pay up to 5.5 percent in contributions, but their pensions are entitlements. Police and fire people pay substantially more in contributions. Union representatives on the board are there to oversee the process, protect the unionized staff members, and be cognizant of the relationship between the state's collective bargaining and the terms and conditions of pension rights and benefits which have changed over the last decade—usually becoming more generous.

State Investment Criteria

To "centralize all functions relating to the purchase, sale or exchange of securities for the state's diverse funds under experienced and professional judgment," P.L. 1950, c. 270 established a New Jersey Division of Investment, a

---

27 Ibid. of 7.
28 Gelinas, Nicole and E.J. McMahon "The Biggest Public Pension Investment Policy Shift You've probably Never Heard Of," *Manhattan Institute*, June 13, 2005.

nine member council, as well as the Director of the Division as the sole overseer and executor of "investment, or reinvestment of moneys of, and purchase, sale or exchange of any investments or securities" for the State of New Jersey's pensions. The duties of the council, pursuant to the 1950 legislation, include the formulation and establishment of investment policy and "from time to time amend, modify or repeal such policies as it may deem proper, which shall govern the methods, practices or procedures for investment, reinvestment, purchase, sale or exchange transactions to be followed by the Director of the Division of Investment established hereunder."[29] Also, all investment proposals from the office of the Director of the Division of Investment were to be regulated by the Treasurer, or by the Investment Council and council members on whose behalf the investment is made.

Four of the nine original council seats were dedicated to representatives of state employees, prison officers, teachers, and police and firemen; the remaining five were to be appointed by the governor based upon investment and finance experience. In 2007 the council was enlarged to 13 seats, four of which are still representatives of the four original agencies legislated in 1950. The two seats added in 2007 are appointed by the Governor from a list of candidates chosen by the AFL-CIO and the New Jersey Education Association. The current council of 13 governs over and represents the interests of seven public pension systems and meets 11 times a year in order to review and discuss new policy and to monitor pension performance. The 13 member council (See appendix 1) is responsible for nominating candidates for director, one of whom is then appointed by the Treasurer.

The power to invest is ultimately left to the discretion of the director who allocates the fund pursuant to the investment policy set by the council. As a measure of accountability, the original legislation requires every director to deposit a bond of $100,000 with the Treasurer upon appointment. The Treasurer or the client agency can reject the director's proposal as long as that rejection is issued in 48 hours. Until 1997, no actual "prudent investment" policy was in place. The "Prudent Investor Act of 1997" that passed into law during Governor Whitman's administration basically eclipsed and loosened the prior standards for investment by shifting all power to execute investment decisions to the Director. As of P.L. 1997 c. 26, the director is held in all investment activity to the broad notion of prudence called the "prudent person" or, properly, the prudent investor standard. New Jersey's notion of prudence takes the "whole portfolio" into account and sees all investments as holistic and instrumental in the investment process, which should be attentive to "diversity, minimiz [ing] risk and improv[ing] returns."[30]

---

29 P.L. 1950 c. 270 sec. 13.

30 Ibid of 20 p. 13.

In contrast to the prudent investor policy adopted by New Jersey in 1997, statutory lists of prudent investments – used in several other municipalities - require "the establishment of express quantitative limits on the types of assets in which pension funds may be invested."[31] Though statutory lists and prudent investor policies are popularly considered to be stark opposites, they are not actually mutually exclusive. This is evidenced by New Jersey's hybrid approach to investment.[32] New Jersey's quantitative allocation limits (See appendix 2) originate in the Investment Council though they might conceivably be legislated in a meeting of elected officials who represent taxpayers. Quantitative limits are not the only factors involved in the investment decisions of the director; recommendations made by the council also positively influence New Jersey's portfolio.

In 2004, Orin Kramer – who had become Investment Council Chair in 2003 — maintained that reforming New Jersey's portfolio in order to avoid similar allocation constellations was among the most important of the council's objectives:

For the three-year period ending in 2002, New Jersey significantly under-performed relative to other pension funds or institutional funds. During the prior three-year period, it significantly outperformed. Historically the risk-adjusted returns are below average. The reason for changing is not that you had three years that under-performed, it's that there was too much risk in the portfolio.[33]

In other words, great risk can lead to higher gains, but also substantial losses. It seems that the chair's goal was to decrease the risk of the portfolio. Was this associated with a decrease in expected return, or was there an expectation that return could be generated with less risk? This is critical because if lower risk implies lower return, then the gap must be made up by increased contributions from employees, employers, or state revenues dedicated

---

31 J. Alan Nelson, "The Prudent Person Rule: A Shield for the Professional Trustee" *Baylor University Law Review*, (Fall 1993): Nelson's is an interesting article follows the national trend of prudent investor legislation and responds to the often ambiguous usage of "prudent person" where "prudent investor" is meant. The prudent investor is one of determining "whether the trustee's primary responsibility if to safeguard the rest of the trust of to generate income." Most relevant to the dilemma of prudency in New Jersey where it was generally accepted that the latter, the generation of income, was the purpose of prudency. Briefly, the author moves through the various faces of this slippery standard of prudence.

32 Galer, Russell. "'Prudent Person' Standard for the Investment of Pension Fund Assets" Organization for Economic and Co-operation and Development, Jan, 2003.

33 Kramer, Orin. "On Diversifying the State's pension Funds" *NJBIZ*. Interview, Nov 2004.

for this purpose. The pension fund can not simply take more risk with the hope of achieving higher yields. This approach leaves the fund vulnerable to the cyclical booms and busts of volatile markets. The fundamental question is whether the return expectations in the portfolio are appropriate for the liabilities over the long run, and if not, is there the political will to match it with contributions or adjustments in benefits. Or is the fund taking on excessive risk to try to keep contributions lower? It seems the fund has begun to move in the right direction with attempts to reduce risk.

Diversification is the key to managing risk. In terms of portfolio management, allocation is a more significant determinant of return than securities selection. In 2007, the target allocation of investments produced by the council was thus:

Total Equities Target: 55.7 percent.
Includes domestic equities, 30.7 percent; international equities in developed markets, 22.5 percent; and international equities in emerging markets, 2.5 percent.
Total Fixed Income Target: 31 percent.
Includes U.S. fixed income, 25 percent; U.S. high yield, 3 percent; and Treasury Inflation-Protected Securities (TIPS), 3 percent.
Alternative Investment Target: 10.3 percent.
Includes private equity, real estate and hedge funds, as well as commodities and other real assets.
Cash Target: 3 percent.[34]

The asset allocation targets are further refined through a process of indexing or targeting a list of benchmarks. The Division of Investment cites the following as reliable sources for the development of sound investment plans:

Standard & Poor's Composite 1500 Index for domestic equities;

The Morgan Stanley Capital International-Europe, Australia and Far East Index (MSCI EAFE ex-Prohibited securities) for international equities;

A blend of the Lehman U.S. Government/Credit and Lehman Long Government/Credit indices for domestic fixed-income;

The HFRI Fund of Funds Composite Index for hedge funds and the National Council of Real Estate Investment Fiduciaries Property Index, NPI, plus 100 basis points for real estate; and

90-day Treasury Bill performance for cash.[35]

In essence, analysts should be guided by sound investment with

---

34 Ibid. of 20
35 Ibid: One source called this practice "veiled indexing."

extensive research, and portfolio managers' reliance should be balanced between stock indexes like that quoted above, and active management of the account. According to Director William Clark, New Jersey's assets are currently distributed among 17 managers, and each manager is responsible for approximately $4.7 billion. Director Clark has described the division's investment as a balance of "top down" or macro-economic management performed by Investment Council members, and "bottom up" or the micro–economic management performed by individual analysts and managers throughout the investment process.[36] However, it seems that the number of staff is too few , and potentially ill-equipped for such great responsibilities. Clark has mentioned that pension funds in most states use outside managers in order to make up staffing shortfalls.

Some critics have questioned why invest state pension funds in uncertain markets or in troubled financial institutions like Lehman Brothers. Why not just put them in treasury bonds? As to why New Jersey does not use a less-risky strategy of investing the pension fund in treasury bonds, the answer is treasury bonds alone cannot produce enough revenue to meet the level of pension liabilities. Simply put, the state cannot afford a very low risk strategy that produces too little in the way of return. However, we have just seen what a large allocation to the stock and corporate bond markets can do.

Pension liability is a fairly fixed or unmoving calculation of cost-of-living, salary, inflation, etc. Because the New Jersey pension fund is so large, it is difficult to increase returns substantially in a very short period of time. Contributions in that time must be either invested and committed to other bonds or stretched over the benefits paid out to employees who retire in the meantime.

State Investment Strategy

Having defined distinct challenges facing the problematic intersection of government pensions and investment, any reform effort should attempt to meet these challenges and better manage the risk of the pension fund's investment portfolio. A simple solution might be to choose a less volatile means of gaining sufficient return, though, as noted in earlier sections of this report, the most stable investment strategies fail to fund even a minimum level of New Jersey's increasing pension liability. Also, there are statutory reforms that need to be enacted to ensure that any future returns, modest or large, are governed by sound fiduciary reasoning. That is, "prudent" investment should mean minimizing risk, rather than maximizing gains. One complication is

---

36 Personal Interview C

that in a more diversified portfolio, if one class of asset allocation yields below expectations, then even more burden falls on the other categories.

Pension fund returns should be first applied to liability, and surpluses should be left to accrue, perhaps, in less lucrative and lower risk investments until formally allocated.

As transparency should shape all processes of government, especially those involving the investment and distribution of public money, the Division of Investment should not only strive to make the details of the investment process more available but also more accessible. However, as the transparency of publicly traded stock means more risk:

Allocation percentages should always be overtly available to New Jerseyans prior to the proposal's passage, as it is with any other legislative issue.

New instruments of analysis should be developed and made available for the purpose of accessing gains in low risk investments and respecting the nature of private equity funds.

The current Director of New Jersey's pension fund, William Clark, has recognized the need for a reform in the investment process.[37] The new management has, in many ways, enacted the most important reforms discussed in this report, including an exploration of private equity, an emphasis on risk, and the importance of diversification, which has been achieved through the increasing use of smaller allocations and investment in systemically diverse foreign markets, most especially Western Europe, Japan, Canada, and Australia.[38]

In 2007, the New Jersey State Division of Investment (SDI) under the State Department of Treasury released a year-end report to detail the activities of New Jersey's pension portfolio and to offer a forward-looking outlook on the recovery of New Jersey's unfunded pension liability. The State Division of Investment, having won the Wall Street Hall of Fame Award for 2008, optimistically reported that diversity, flexibility, and foreign investment would mark its strategy going into the next fiscal year.

The SDI claims that a strategy of alternative investment will save New Jersey pensions from various market pitfalls such as those that befell the pension fund when too much of its assets were allocated to common equities during the dot-com build up. The SDI reports that it was wary of

---

37 Ibid. of 20.

38 The authors of this paper have investigated the question of politically driven divestment from foreign markets. In the past, administrations in New Jersey have prohibited investment in Northern Ireland, South Africa, and Darfur. Based upon our investigations and interviews, the differences in yield as a result of political divestment from foreign markets are unclear; William Clark Memo, Nov 11, 2008.

the mortgage boom that began as a consequence of dot-com fall out, and therefore avoided too many risky investments in unstable mortgages. The SDI offers the observation that when compared to similar investment portfolios in other and similar states, those who diversified "into other asset classes, have significantly out-performed New Jersey on a risk-adjusted basis over five-, 10- and 15- year periods – and that performance was attributable to superior asset allocation policies."[39] The SDI has therefore applied this observation to the allocation process.

Among the changes made to the way pensions are managed, the State Investment Council (SIC) or the policy arm of the SDI, recommended an emphasis on international investments and, likewise, a lowered emphasis on domestic investment.[40] This policy change is intended to reduce risk by investing in markets ruled by forces that are characteristically different from domestic or American markets—or at least were in late 2008. By investing in emerging overseas markets, not only do investments offset somewhat the recent and ongoing uncertainties of U.S. markets, but there is also a greater chance of growth as new industries and countries have recently begun a period of strong development. The accumulation of assets in non-North American nations is substantial.

Another important reform to New Jersey pension policy is the SIC's recommendation that there be less emphasis on public equity funds—which is responsible for the majority of New Jersey's investments—and more emphasis on private equity funds, "the only new asset class in the portfolio expected to out-perform public equities over the long-term."[41] Real estate was considered, and hedge funds "as a means to generate positive returns that have a low correlation to public equities" were also perceived to be promising new asset classes to add to New Jersey's portfolio.[42]

In line with the migration from public equities to private equity funds and hedge funds, the SDI notes, "In recognition of the fact that the plan's liabilities are long-term in nature, we've sought to extend the duration (i.e. the average maturity) of the fund's fixed income portfolio from roughly five to more than ten years."[43] However, without taking on significant credit risk, bonds lock in yields that are below the expectation of the overall fund. So that drag on performance must be made up somewhere.

The pension fund, being so large, is perhaps too much temptation for politicians. The former liquidity and concentration of New Jersey's investments

39 Ibid. of 20.
40 Ibid of 20.
41 Ibid. of 20.
42 Ibid of 20.
43 Ibid of 20.

was dangerous in this regard. Pensions, being money entrusted to the state by the public, must be protected from this kind of danger. Ultimately, New Jersey's new financial strategy moves some of its investment into less liquid equity funds, though greater commitment is still not as binding or unproductive as investing in bonds with fixed rates of interest.

Since they are guaranteed by the state, individual pensioners are never in absolute danger of losing their assets. The pension fund, however, is vulnerable. Therefore, the competent management of pensions is more of a protection for taxpayers, who often must unfairly foot the bill. With an effort to keep and increase the transparency of the investment process and increased contributions, the New Jersey pension fund may one day have a surplus –at which point New Jersey taxpayers may benefit.

Changing Strategies

Historically, the pension fund was invested largely in common stocks and bonds.[44] In 1991, the Investment Council authorized investment in international stock and bonds; from 1995 to 1999, New Jersey's pension plan returned an average of 27.96 percent per year, ranking it among the top of all public pension funds in that period. But after 2001, the value of the fund dropped by $14 billion in just two years, and because the pension fund was not significantly diversified, it suffered extensively when the stock market declined during the dot-com bubble burst. The McGreevey Administration wisely made a movement toward diversification into alternative investments. In recent years, the two major unions—the CWA and the NJEA—opposed moving management of these funds from in-house employees to outsiders.[45] That outsourcing would allow less volatile returns as the assets would be under the constant care of private equity, hedge fund, and real estate managers who are thought to "add value" and performance to the portfolios they manage by delivering absolute versus relative performance. One complication to investing with these managers is transparency as private equity and hedge fund managers often keep information about their clients and portfolios confidential.

In general, the Investment Council did transfer funds to private equity and hedge funds,[46] and to some real estate investments. The Council summarizes the changes, which began in 2003:

A significant reduction in the allocation in domestic equities to reduce

---

44 Ibid. of 21.
45 Personal interview A & D
46 Ibid of 20.

risk, which slightly increases the allocations in international equities, partially those in so called emerging market countries.

Initiating investments in private equity.

Initiating investments in real estate.

Initiating investments in hedge funds.

Initiating an inflation sensitive portfolio.

Extend plan's liabilities from five to more than ten years.

That policy shift was indeed a correct one. The movement has been from two to five to seven classes of investments. Some have compared New Jersey to New York and California. The major advantages that California and New York State have are they were more diversified earlier, and have a more robust and better-compensated staff, which has access to many more sources of information and tools to make investment decisions and allocations. Staff in New Jersey have to submit to a difficult and inefficient procedure just to buy the information tools that they need to perform due diligence, to go to conferences in order to upgrade their work skills, and even to travel to New York City to attend investment prospecting meetings.[47]

In making decisions, the State Investment Council exercises its own policy judgment subject to state statutes and regulations from the state Treasury department that limit discretion.[48] The ethics code that governs the Treasury Department also applies to the Investment staff.

This small staff (only about 70 people) should be managing the managers, not making allocation decisions itself. But this is complicated by a recent Supreme Court decision, which curtailed the delegation of investment decisions to non-state entities.[49] Although they are responsible for enormous amounts of funds, very few people in each division or area of the investment section have sufficient staff and analysts.[50] These middle managers and assets managers need to have performance expectations and a reward structure that matches more closely the best of the other public funds and the better private endowments. The state has reached a point where these positions can no longer be bound by of the benefits and entitlements of the regular personnel system. Unions as well as taxpayers have, of course, substantial vested interests in the huge pension fund in New Jersey. There is still substantial criticism in union ranks of the investment policies of Governor Florio and especially Governor Whitman. But the current staffing and resources may create a situation in which too much risk is taken, since many staffers do not have time, staff, or

---

47   Personal interview A
48   Personal Interview A,C,D,E
49   Personal Interview A,C,D,E
50   Personal interview A

the computer systems to follow the large number of securities already in the portfolio – or perhaps deserving to be added to the portfolio.[51]

Transparency in the Public System

While the state avoided owning any Freddie Mac or Fannie Mae common stock, there has been much criticism of the decision to invest 1.5 percent of the fund's then assets in the stock of Lehman Brothers just weeks before the company filed for bankruptcy. Director Clark argues that there was no such knowledge of the imminent failure of Lehman , and Lehman stock traded above $28 a share on the day of the New Jersey purchase.[52] In the wake of the investment decision and the subsequent total loss of the money invested, a number of sources familiar with the New Jersey State Investment Council's decision to invest in Lehman Brothers were asked why one would make this sort of investment. In conducting the research for this report, we found that in fact there were two different investments in Lehman—a second one after its problems became even more apparent. Asked for an explanation as to how this happened, our sources offered these responses: New Jersey wasn't the only investment fund to make that mistake, and the New Jersey fund was guided by the so-called "discipline of the market" where Lehman stock was still being traded. One critic, however, has argued that New Jersey was knowingly taking part in a bailout strategy for Lehman.[53] Though Director Clark vigorously insists that the decision to invest in Lehman was made by his staff in accordance with normal investment procedure,[54] not by the Investment Council, some newspaper columnists and politicians charge[55] that Investment Council members had links to the failed Wall Street investment bank. Several members of the Investment Council were previously employed by Lehman (See appendix 1). This report includes biographical sketches of the public members of the council.

Some of our sources argue that the Lehman management opportunity

---

51 Personal interview A
52 Personal interview D, B, & C; William Clark, Memo, Nov 11, 2008.
53 Personal interview D
54 Personal interview E
55 Ibid. of 28& Personal interviews D & E.; *wallstreetweather.net*, accessed: 10/22/2008; David Voreacos and Linda Standler, "Lehman said to be Subpoenaed on Claims to Investors" *bloomberg.com*, accessed 10/22/2008; Hui-Yong Yu and Adam Cataldo, "New Jersey Pension fund lost 450m on Lehman," *bloomberg.com*, accessed 10/22/2008; Lisa G. Ryan, "Why did N.J. Pension System Loose So Much Money with Lehman Bros." *Daily Record. com*, accessed 10/22/2008.

was offered to a select few people. However, still others believe that the investment was made without the appropriate due diligence. Director Clark, however, argues that it was not a private placement investment but was in public stock.[56]

One of the sources for confusion is the role of the Investment Council and the role of the director. Our research indicates that the Investment Council sets the asset allocation policy for the overall portfolio, as shown on pages 14 and 15. The director is also required to seek board approval for investments over $50 million in the alternative decisions. So the Lehman investment would be part the common stock allocation designated by the council -- and completely left to the judgment of the staff and the director. Thus despite its size, it would not require board approval because it was not an alternative investment. However, an investment like this could very well have been conducted on a "private" basis in which it may not fit under the existing allocation. Could it have been done as a private investment in a public company or as some type alternative investment where potentially there could have been more due diligence undertaken? In these tumultuous times, we believe a review of responsibilities and greater transparency are warranted. Furthermore, it is our understanding that the investment in Lehman was accompanied by a decrease in other correlated financial institution investments that subsequently experienced significant losses. As a result, the loss in Lehman, though making headlines, did not take place in a vacuum. The overall loss to New Jersey would have been greater if the state had not decreased its investments in these other correlated financial institutions at the same time it was investing in Lehman. The real destruction of the value of the fund comes from the asset allocation to common equities, and to some extent corporate bonds.

Those close to the workings of the SIC argue that the council makes only policy decisions, with its staff making and allocating the investments. But in fact, in the Fall of 2008, the Newhouse newspapers reported that the decision to discuss the investment of $94 million in an attempt to assist hedge fund BlackRock was made by the SIC. Apparently not all members of the council agreed with the decision. CWA member Jim Marketti worried about compounding the state's losses: "It's worked out differently than was originally proposed. The investments they made were paying 85 cents on the dollar, now they're worth 65 cents on a dollar. Now they're trying to sell us on the grounds that 65 cents is a great investment." Mr. Marketti has expressed concern that the state is throwing good money after bad. We point to a distinction in that the investment may very well lose money, but that is not necessarily throwing good after bad. The real question is whether the allocation is the best allocation of capital given what the investment council and staff knows at

---

56 Personal Interview A; William Clark Memo, Nov 11, 2008.

the time. And if it is, then the investment should be made. If not, the capital should be allocated somewhere else. The chair of the Council, Orin Kramer, has said that the bank loans that BlackRock invests in are much safer than common stock. This statement is true, but how do they fit into the overall asset allocation? Are they in place of the common stock allocation, or are they an increase in the hedge fund allocation? And if so, should the fund further reduce common equities to add more of the safer bank loans? State Treasury spokesman, Tom Vincz, predicted the investments would get a 20 percent return.[57] We believe that the Investment Council and staff should, and likely will, reconsider the overall asset allocation given the enormous dislocations in the markets.

Later news stories led to some more criticisms and complexities. The Senate President, Richard Codey, questioned why $49.5 million was put in the hedge fund on October 17 — an amount barely under the $50 million threshold that requires a review by the State Investment Council. Then on October 31, the state invested another $94 million in BlackRock. BlackRock had asked its investors, including the New Jersey fund, to increase stakes by 36 percent so it could avoid selling some of its holdings. At first BlackRock said it would accept $49.5 million in October, and then wait until the Investment Council meeting in mid November for the rest. But BlackRock subsequently insisted it needed the full amount by October 31, requiring an emergency meeting. In September 2007, New Jersey had invested its first $400 million when the loans were trading at 90 cents on the dollar; the loans are now trading at 70 cents on the dollar.

Senator Codey argued that an investment of that size needed to be reviewed, but the Investment Council and Treasury officials disagreed. Governor Corzine indicated that he opposed the Legislature getting involved in examining investment policies and allocations.

The issue of transparency has become even more confusing as illustrated in this case. The Executive Director and the council spokespeople have vigorously insisted that the basic 1950 law's division of responsibilities is being honored. The Executive Director manages the fund; the council sets policy but stays out of particular investment decisions. But surely from the statements of Mr. Marketti it appears that members of the council thought they were being asked to approve the allocation. Despite the BlackRock allocations, Investment Director Clark and Vincz have still maintained that the council does not technically approve investments of any size. Vincz maintains, "This

---

57   Dunstan McNichol. "State bolsters hedge fund." *The Times of Trenton,* Nov 1, 2008. P.1.

is procurement, it's not an approval process. It's a presentation process so they are aware of it and there is transparency with the public as well.[58]

Too often public funds, especially large ones as in New Jersey's case, do not exercise enough good due diligence in terms of research, analysis, and critical judgments when it comes to making investment decisions. We urge that the administration and the Legislature examine other large state pension funds and also private endowments of colleges, universities, and museums. In the New York Times of April 15, 2009, in an article dealing with investing in hedge funds Director William Clark remarked, "Clearly, it did not work out as well as we had hoped, and expected. You cannot deny that as a general asset class, it didn't deliver what investors were led to believe." Union representative on the Board, Jim Marketti, concluded that the state fund has not moved cautiously enough into hedge funds. "If we had invested it in the mattress, we would have done better," he concluded. But Orin Kramer defended the investments, saying hedge funds did better than the stock market. "But even in 2008, hedge funds reduced volatility and were better places to be than these stocks [referring to auto companies, banks and home building companies]."[59]

Conclusion

This is the first in a series of Hall Institute papers on the investment of state pension funds. It was conducted as a first response to the debate that has intensified given the well publicized investment in Lehman and BlackRock and the ensuing criticisms. As always , the Institute welcomes debate on this topic and on any of our conclusions. We believe this will be a significant topic in the months to come. It needs to be studied thoughtfully, and we hope that it can be done in a bipartisan manner without sensationalism driven by politics. That is not to say that there are not reasonable criticisms, sharp differences in opinions, or significant changes that should be made.

The strategy for the investment of the New Jersey state pension fund is now a hybrid in which some of the fund investments are made directly by the staff, while some are allocated to outside managers. The investments made internally are primarily in stocks, bonds and cash consistent with the

---

58   Dunstan McNichol and Claire Heininger. "Governor: Loosen the Fiscal Leash Legislators Calling For a Say in Investments." *Star Ledger* Nov 4, 2008; Claire Heininger. "Official Defends $144M Decision Denies Charge By Codey The Move Avoided Review." *The Star Ledger,* Nov 3, 2008.

59   Personal Interview A; Leslie Wayne, "Public Pension Managers Rethink Hedge Fund Ties," *New York Times*, April 15, 2009, B1, 5.

asset allocation direction of the SDI. The investments allocated to outside managers are in alternative investments, specifically hedge funds, real estate and private equity.

From history, New Jersey has learned that public money should not be surrendered to the will of current market trends, which are often characterized by cyclical booms and busts. Likewise, investment policy should certainly emphasize risk management and "prudence," not just expected return. As public markets are at the mercy of a capricious and unfocused multitude of personal interests, it may not be considered "prudent" to invest large amounts of New Jersey's important pension contributions in them. However, then the contribution and benefit structure needs to be re examined. Or since New Jersey's investments are merely a wealth accumulation tool with objectives that are long term in nature, there should be a long term focus on what the real expected return of various asset classes are and how that fits into the long term objectives of the fund. They should therefore not be surrendered to politicians and council members with limited tenures and goals that are too often short-sighted. This history is especially apparent in New Jersey where six governors, beginning with and including Governor Florio, have served relatively short tenures. Only one Governor of the six, Governor Whitman, was elected to a second term.

Asset management is the most competitive business in the world, so competitive that a great deal of academic literature as well as many practitioners believe it is impossible to beat the market, and therefore investors should give up and just index. If the fund were to index, then it would be a very low cost operation and the key to its success would be based on the allocation of capital which is decided by the Investment Council. Under this scenario, the staff probably could be reduced to purely administrative positions given that indexing does not require any top down or bottom up analysis but simply investing in all the components of the index or outsourcing to an index manager at very low cost. This is a theoretically acceptable way to manage a portfolio. However, we must understand that over the long run, this has two risks:

The return may not be great enough to keep up with the benefits provided, and therefore contributions will have to be increased. Given the allocation that the Investment Council currently has, it is unlikely that it can keep up with the benefits provided.

The long run returns may be quite different than the short run returns in markets that have booms and busts. The real danger here is that during booms the state has a tendency to neglect contributions because of a feeling of security that quickly evaporates during bear markets and cycles like the one we are in now.

So any decision to deviate from indexing is based upon the belief that active management will produce returns that are superior to the index. Regardless of whether this is done internally or externally, it will cost more than indexing. We believe that active management is important for a large pension fund because, if done properly, active management can produce outsize returns with lower risk. We also believe there is the potential for success using internal as well as external managers. However we are not convinced that New Jersey has the appropriate framework.

Our conclusion is that the fund should be actively managed through the use of both internal and external managers. But there must be some conditions. First, for internal active management, there must be the necessary tools, people and process. We believe this can be improved in New Jersey. This includes research, technology, computer systems and the appropriate personnel similar to the private sector. Second, there must be coordination between what is managed inside and what is managed outside. Too many funds have "buckets" of different types of investment and different consultants and outside management for each bucket. Unfortunately the different sectors are interrelated and correlated and sometimes this may not be coordinated. Use of outside managers is appropriate for many strategies where there is a specific niche, or expertise that is too prohibitive to be built internally. Then the use of external managers is justified. However, it is incumbent upon the fund itself to have some transparency into the risk of each manager's strategy so that it can be factored into the overall portfolio risk of the fund. This includes allocation of underlying assets as well as leverage.

This approach creates a dilemma for a public fund where there is resistance to paying what one could earn in the private sector, and a similar reluctance to pay outside managers. However, how else can a fund compete? The Institute notes the fact that there are some public and endowment positions which are filled with the best personnel earning far less than they could make in the private sector. These institutions are fortunate to have the "philanthropy" of such public servants. However, such positions still must have the support and prestige needed to attract such a people. We believe New Jersey has attracted some very good people, but should focus on further creating and enhancing an environment where the best people want to work, or continue to work, and where they have the tools necessary for success.

As for recent headlines, we do not have any bias given the loss in Lehman Brothers. We believe that it was done with the best of intentions and hopes, and we understand that investments lose money. However we believe that questions dealing with the process and transparency are legitimate. But many of the criticisms are not quite accurate.

It has been said by Director Clark that there was reliance on the market pricing as valuation for Lehman Brothers. What seems not to be reported is that since this was an investment in a public equity and qualified under the 55 percent common stock allocation set by the council, it was actually replacing other financial sector stocks that were sold at the time. Those financial stocks had they remained in the portfolio would have lost a significant amount, maybe close to as much as the Lehman investment lost. So the net to the portfolio may not have been that significant. Of much greater importance is the overall risk embedded in the common stock portfolio.

However, an alternative view is that Lehman was a investment. And such investments may be appropriate for the pension funds if the analysis can be done and if it has a compelling risk reward. A one off investment in a struggling brokerage firm may be a good investment, but it is not clear how it fits into the asset allocation direction of the SDI. Clearly it is a common equity, but it is unique enough that it may be inconsistent with the 55 percent common equity bucket using the S&P as an index. But, if it is looked at similar to a private investment, truly evaluating such an investment can only be done by taking non-public information and doing an analysis that a private equity firm may do. We do not believe New Jersey has allocated enough resources to this analysis. We also are not privy to how the investment was sourced. There have been suggestions that there are conflicts, but we have no evidence of that.

Recently, there was also a newsworthy investment in BlackRock. Given the turmoil in the market, additional equity was invested to stave off margin calls. Clearly margin calls and forced selling are not to the advantage of the owner, but there is always the risk that good money goes after bad. We see no evidence that the investment in BlackRock was not appropriate. However, the negative press and public perception could have been avoided by a more transparent process. There seems to be some confusion as to what the role of the Investment Council was. It seemed to be involved in BlackRock but not in Lehman. This is the part of the process that remains unclear and needs to be clearer to avoid questions and criticisms

In late November, it was reported that the pension fund invested in two other hedge funds with amounts of $49.5 million each.[60] This is the area where we have some concern. Is $49.5 million the appropriate allocation? Why not $60 million? Or $25 million? If it is a compelling investment, was it limited because of an arbitrary rule? This we find to be inappropriate. There can be investments of $25 million that have far more risk than investments of $100 million. So why the arbitrary cutoff of $50 million? We believe that the SDI should be involved in any investment that is not typical of the fund and has

---

60   Dunstan McNichol. "State money went to 2 additional hedge funds. *Star Ledger,* Nov 23, 2008

unique risks, not just the size. As with BlackRock, we believe during these difficult times the atmosphere is ripe for doubts and bad publicity. Making investments just under some arbitrary number is food for criticism that is not helpful to anyone. We believe this rule should be reconsidered and the role of the council more clearly defined.

Finally, in regard to the issue of conflicts, we believe that one must be careful about conflicts of interest and the only way to give comfort is for accountability, transparency and fair judgment of performance against appropriate benchmarks.

New Jersey is suffering along with the rest of the world in this debacle. However, there are incredible opportunities to take advantage of this situation for the future. We believe that to do this, decisions must be rational and not emotional. Most importantly, the return will be determined by the asset allocation mix. We believe this needs to be studied and potentially adjusted given all the dislocations in the market. Then there must be an analysis of the expected return over long periods and a comparison to the long run liabilities of the fund. There must be significant attention paid to the contributions that will be needed to fund any shortfalls. Taxpayers bear responsibility and they should be represented. Finally, any reductions in contributions, as recently suggested by the Governor, should be done in conjunction with a long run plan for funding the liabilities. This approach requires a great deal of coordination and research, so it is critical for all of the components to be harmonized.

The Hall Institute is hopeful that our examination of New Jersey's pension investment system leads to debate and discussion that will improve the process. We look forward to working cooperatively with all interested parties and stakeholders to ensure that this most important goal is attained.

CHAPTER 2 • APPENDIX 1

Council Member Biographies

Orin S. Kramer, Chair
General Partner
Boston Provident, L.P.

Orin Kramer is a General Partner of Boston Provident LP. He also serves as Chairman of the New Jersey State Investment Council. He was previously associated with the management consulting firm of McKinsey & Company; the law firm of Simpson Thacher & Bartlett; and the White House Domestic Policy Staff under President Carter.

Jonathan Berg, Vice Chair
Representing
Public Employees' Retirement System

Jonathan Berg has been employed by the New Jersey Department of Environmental Protection since April of 1979. He is a graduate of Richard Stockton State College (now known as Richard Stockton College of New Jersey), class of 1979, and holds a B.S. in Environmental Science. He has been an elected member of the Executive Board of Communications Workers of America (CWA) Local 1034 for 5 consecutive 3-year terms as Vice-President, Higher Level Supervisory Unit. His last term expires December 31, 2008.

Erika Irish Brown

Former Senior Vice President of Diversity Lateral Recruiting of Lehman Brothers, Inc., Erika Irish Brown chairs the Investment Council's Diversity Committee, a committee formed for the purpose of providing continual evaluation of the Council's regulations and policies to promote diversity in broker and manager relationships. Ms. Brown has worked as Senior Vice President for Business Development of Black Entertainment Television (BET) through Viacom; Director of the Bedford Stuyvesant Restoration Corporation.

Maj. Marshall C. Brown
Representing

State Police Retirement System

W. Montgomery Cerf
Managing Director
Barclays Capital

Former Managing Director at Lehman Brothers, Inc. Currently Managing Director of Barclay's Capital. Former managing director in charge of North American institutional sales, marketing and investor relations at Lehman Brothers until December 2006. Mr. Cerf is currently managing director and senior banker at JPMorgan.

Jose R. Claxton
Director
Latigo Partners, L.P.

James Clemente
Representing

Teachers' Pension and Annuity Fund

Susan Ann Crotty
Managing Director

Tremont Capital Management

Mark Kandrac
Representing
Police & Firemen's Pension Fund Board

Mr. Kandrac represents the Police & Firemen's Pension Fund Board and is currently Platoon Captain of the Hamilton Township Fire District No. 2.

James C. Kellogg
President
J.C. Kellogg Foundation

James Kellogg is President of the Community Foundation of New Jersey, was a partner in the law firm of Townley and Updike based in Manhattan, was a member of the Finance Committee for Meridian Health Systems, former board member of The Prudential Insurance Company of America, past President of Children's Specialized Hospital in Mountainside, former board member of New Jersey Housing and Mortgage Finance Agency, the Council of the Woodrow Wilson School at Princeton University and the Scholarship Fund for Inner City Children and served on the Committee of Financial Affairs and Physical Plant of the Bloomfield College Board of Trustees. He graduated From Princeton University and Harvard Law School.

Douglas A. Love, PhD
Chief Investment Officer
Ryan Labs, Inc.

Dr. Love is Chief Investment Officer at Ryan Labs, Inc., New York; was the Founder and former Chairman of Buck Investment Services; has been a consultant to the PBGC and World Bank; has participated in Financial Accounting Standards deliberations; served as Chairman of the Employee Benefits Research Institute; has been project manager for the Council of Economic Advisors for the White House; and was a member of the Grace Commission. Dr. Love has taught at both New York University and Rutgers business schools. He has a BME from Cornell University, an MBA from New York University and a PhD in Economics from Columbia University.

Vacant
Representing
New Jersey State AFL-CIO

Vacant
Representing
The New Jersey Education Association

Chapter 2 • Appendix 2

The following is a list of asset allocation regulations released in a treasury report from 2000:

STATE INVESTMENT COUNCIL
REGULATORY POLICY DECISION FOR THE PENSION FUNDS

- Equity investment must be no more than 70 percent of the portfolio, including both international and domestic equities.
- International investment is limited to 22 percent of the portfolios, including both international stocks and bonds.
- International investment in both stocks and bonds is limited to countries that have at least one AA sovereign rating.
- All international investments may be hedged through currency transactions.
- Equity real estate investment is limited to 10 percent of the portfolio; however, investment in this area is restricted to REITs due to regulatory limitations.
- Unlimited investment is permitted in securities of U.S. Government and designated agencies. CMOs are limited by internal policy.
- Investment in domestic corporate bonds is limited to companies with a rating of Baa/BBB or better.
- Investment by the pension funds in mortgages is defined as pools of certain specified government agencies, with one regulation permitting investment in pools of conventional mortgages with specific credit guidelines.
- Investments in municipal bonds, commercial paper, repurchase agreements, certificates of deposits, bankers acceptances, etc. are all permitted by specific regulations that specify high credit standards and conservative investment limits.
- All investments in any one security are limited to a portion of the security issue, and thus all investments require co-investment ensuring diversification and market pricing.

CHAPTER 2 • APPENDIX 3

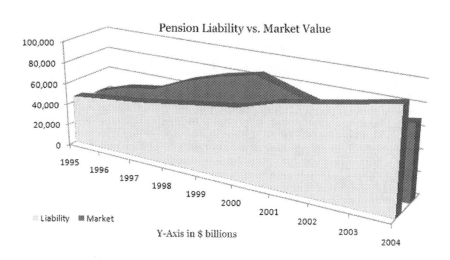

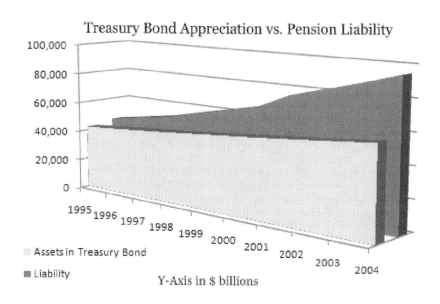

Pensions Invested in Treasury Bonds at a Rate of 7.25 Percent

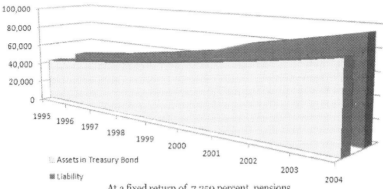

At a fixed return of 7.250 percent, pensions
still fail to meet liability by 15.4 billion.

CHAPTER THREE

RECOMMENDATIONS AND GUIDANCE FOR PENSION REFORM

By
Michael P. Riccards

The problems confronting New Jersey's public pension and benefit system are not new. What has been lacking has been the courage and willingness to tackle a problem with solutions that are so politically untenable.

Since our inception in 2005, the Hall Institute of Public Policy – New Jersey has followed the pension issue closely. As state lawmakers begin the difficult task of reforming the system, we offer a few observations and suggestions quelled from our research on this topic.

For starters, at the start of the 2009 fiscal year, the full liability of the state pension fund was about $125.8 billion, of which $34.4 billion was unfunded. In order to make up such a large gap, either higher contributions from state employees and/or government levels, or very significant investment returns are needed.

Based on our review and research, we believe that the management structures that once served the system need to be seriously re-examined. The extreme volatility of the market, the difficulties being faced by non-American markets, the loss of major players in the financial industry, and the much more intrusive role of the government in the market all have led to an environment we have not seen before.

It is our view that the investment process undertaken by the fund management must be made more transparent. Conflicts need to be avoided. It appears that there has been a serious alienation between the State Investment Council and some senior staff members. The responsibilities of the director of the Division of Investments, the staff, consultants, and the council need to be more clearly defined. There should be a general agreement among council members and the director on investment strategy, the role of public and employee contributions, and the overall goals of the fund. New members should have to go through an orientation process focusing on goals and strategies.

The state needs to invest more in upgrading the investment resources available to the director while creating a new tier of trained and experienced asset managers. We believe that there should be an allocation of assets to investment managers who have skills or niches outside what state government employees can demonstrate. And for assets that are managed internally, they should be indexed or managed by capable managers with the requisite expertise and resources. We also believe that there must be a genuine recognition of what various levels of investment risk can achieve over the long run, and how that influences levels of benefits and contributions. Finally, we believe that there needs to be a clear recognition that the long-run perspective for investment returns is far longer than that of any gubernatorial administration, and that adjustments to contributions based on swings in markets, positive or negative, must be avoided.

The Investment Council relies heavily on a staff of professionals who are responsible for enormous investments in the portfolio. As in many public systems, the compensation for staff members is low considering the vast scope of their responsibilities. It is not desirable that these managers be restricted by the state employment system; rather they should have expectations and rewards that are more in line with other public investment agencies and private endowments. The state should examine an enhanced compensation package for the staff, and should be able to recruit based upon this. There are many talented individuals who would work in the appropriate environment with reasonable pay and resources. Employment policies should be amended to pay for – and value – ongoing professional training. The staff also needs help. It needs greater depth in its personnel ranks to analyze and perform due diligence on the ever changing criteria involved in investment policy.

Lastly, the major unions who have so much at stake in the process and in the general solvency of the state government should be more willing to support the prudent and flexible use of outside asset managers by the State Investment Council and the staff. The selection of managers should be given great care, free of conflict and very transparent. It should also fit into a well-defined and coordinated asset allocation process. There may be certain higher costs in managing this portfolio than in the past — but in the end these investments are critical to the state's future. Furthermore, money can be saved through indexing portions of the portfolio rather than random in house management.

From a structural standpoint, a more focused and unified approach on the part of the State Investment Council is in order. It is proposed that the Legislature reconstitute a council made up of nine members, with seven public members chosen by the Governor and ratified by the state Senate. The seven public members will include the state Treasurer (not a designee) and six members chosen for a five-year term, staggered as the Governor sees fit. The other two members of the Council will be chosen from employee unions in a manner the membership chooses. Further, the Council should be given clear objectives for the Fund. Such objectives should possibly be created based upon a task force that could be convened to study the Fund and create reasonable risk reward objectives.

In terms of investment policy, the Investment Council has oversight responsibility for the investments, and the consultants are advisors in the investment process. There should be in the council staff a special office of foreign investments to follow the markets in different time zones. Any funds that are divided up among outside consultants should be allocated on criteria in terms of investment areas. The council should conduct yearly assessments of the performance of each fund manager, and drop the poorest performing investment group. The council will should set aside up to 10 percent of the assets for prudent mortgages and capital for investment in small and/or developing companies. If New Jersey will not invest in its own people, we cannot expect out-of-state sources to invest in us.

The tremendous changes in investment strategies, the volatile market, the speed at which allocations are made, and the increased demands on the fund all require a clear and coordinated strategy for the state. These structural and policy changes will position the state to respond more effectively in the future.

CHAPTER FOUR

TO ENCOURAGE SAVING FOR RETIREMENT, USE RESEARCH TO INFORM POLICY

By
Linda Stamato

Sometimes, it's refreshing to note, research does have an impact on policy. A broad new initiative by the Obama Administration—to make it easier to save for retirement—demonstrates how it can work. After all, academic research can illuminate public problems in ways that can both enhance understanding and answer difficult questions. It can provide insight, moreover, that is essential to good public policy.

What is the initiative? How will it work? And what research informs this plan and policy?

Tax-advantaged retirement accounts

To encourage savings, the Administration has undertaken a number of initiatives to encourage systematic saving: creating automatic enrollment plans; providing an option to receive U.S. savings bonds in lieu of tax refunds; and allowing the 'contribution' of unused vacation time and overtime to retirement accounts.

Mercifully, none required new legislation from Congress.

Earlier, as part of the federal budget, the president included two other proposals to promote savings: one compels all but the smallest employers to offer retirement savings plans and the other expands the saver's tax credit, which matches a family's savings up to $1,000 a year.

Sources of funds to encourage savings? Among them, potentially, are tax returns which, in cash, amount to about $2,000 annually--there are 100,000,000 million tax refunds every year--and, cash that employers routinely provide to workers for their unused vacation and overtime.

Why this initiative?

Savings are critical to the economy. The rate of savings in the nation, even before the recession hit, was bottoming out even as credit card debt was increasing. The habit of saving, moreover, had been turned on its head. In the several decades following World War II, for example, the nation's annual savings set-aside hovered at about 9 percent. People saved to spend; but by the 1990s, people borrowed to spend.

As Roger Lowenstein points out in "The Way We Live Now: U.S. Savings Bind" Americans owned 425 million credit cards in 2008 (that number is down to 344 million now). Instead of plowing savings into stocks and bonds and forming a pool of capital for investments and new technologies, as Americans had done in the post-war years--begetting a golden era of productivity and growth--personal savings rates declined. Credit became more widely available and people became used to borrowing for what they needed (and wanted).

The Obama Administration wanted to reverse that trend and promote saving, and, particularly, saving for retirement. Why the latter? Less that half the work force has access to a retirement plan at work. And, fewer than 10 percent of those without workplace retirement plans have one of their own. So, to push for retirement savings was wise public policy.

How did the Obama Administration know what to do? The simple answer: It's what the research says to do.

What research informs this policy initiative?

The question at the heart is the following: How does (or can) society encourage positive behavior? Should government attempt to affect certain decision-making behaviors? What techniques and tools of science, particularly cognitive science, are likely to steer people toward better choices?

Richard Thaler, a pioneer in the field of cognitive and decision science, and author, with Cass Sunstein, of Nudge: Improving Decisions About Health, Wealth, and Happiness (Yale University Press, 2008), conducted research on consumer savings patterns that has direct relevance. Thaler found that many more people saved money in a 401(K) retirement plan if they did not have to take active steps to join the plan. In one study, only 45 percent of a company's new employees participated in the 401(K) plan when doing so required them to take some kind of action, like filling out a form. However, 86 percent participated when doing so was the default option. People need a "nudge" to act in their own interest.

And, Max Bazerman, along with colleagues at the Harvard Business School, investigated how people make unwise tradeoffs. One finding is particularly relevant. It's this: Most people accept the default position, the status quo. It is not that people are deciding not to do something, they may not be thinking about it and, as a result, they don't take the initiative. They may fail to act in their own best interest.

There really is a difference in how a choice is presented.

President Obama campaigned on the goal of expanding the national savings rate. By the initiatives he has put into place to encourage the nation to save, he has kept his promise. But it was the research that showed him the way.

Linda Stamato is Faculty Fellow and Co-Director, Center for Negotiations and Conflict Resolutions, Rutgers University,
Edward J. Bloustein School of Planning and Public Policy.

CHAPTER FIVE

THE FINANCIAL CRISIS: ORIGINS AND CONSEQUENCES

By
Gerald P. O'Driscoll, Jr.

The economic historian Anna Schwartz has described the recent housing bubble as a classic "mania." She observes that, while the details change in each historical episode, in this case as in others "the basic propagator was too-easy monetary policy and too-low interest rates."[1] In the housing boom, easy money and cheap credit financed an unsustainable increase in investment in residential real estate. Especially in the hottest real estate markets, buying took on a frenzied aspect.

Here, I will first present a brief history of the current economic crisis. Financial services are highly regulated, yet the regulatory system failed. Then, I offer a diagnosis of the crisis, focusing on the issue of the capital position of banks and other financial institutions. Finally, I consider the way forward and the prospects for a return to a sound financial system and a healthy economy.

Origins of the Crisis

During the run-up in home prices, credit was easy, whether measured by its price or by its terms. The nation's central bank, the Federal Reserve System, pegs the Fed funds rate that banks charge each other for the overnight loans of reserves used to fund loans to the public. From November 2001 to December 2004 the Fed funds rate was at or below 2 percent. From June 2003 to June 2004 the rate remained at 1 percent. For much of this period, real (inflation-adjusted) short-term rates of interest were negative. In other words, amounts of money to be repaid in the future would be worth less than what was borrowed due to inflation. It literally paid to borrow money, especially to finance an appreciating asset like residential housing in overheated markets in California, Nevada, Arizona, and Florida. Professor John Taylor of Stanford University has argued that the Fed pushed short-term interest rates below levels predicted by an economic model of monetary policy based on historical patterns (the "Taylor Rule").[2] This episode of easy credit can also be put in historical perspective. There was no central bank in the United States until 1913. But the Bank of England was founded in 1694. After the end of the Napoleonic wars and postwar economic recovery, Great Britain enjoyed nearly a century of peace and prosperity under the gold standard, free international trade, and free movements of capital. It was the Pax Britannica. Prices ended the period roughly where they began.

What was Britain's Bank Rate (the rough equivalent of today's Fed funds rate)? In June 1822, it was 4 percent, and on July 30, 1914, the eve of the First World War, the Bank Rate was 4 percent. At no point in this remarkable period did the Bank Rate ever fall below 2 percent.[3] For the Fed to have set rates so low for so long flew in the face of historical experience and common sense.

There is no rigid relationship between the Fed funds rate and long-term interest rates. But the housing boom was not financed with long-term funds. The days of thirty-year fixed-rate mortgages financed with long-term money were over. There were one-year adjustable-rate mortgages (ARMs) with "teaser rates" for the first two or three years of a mortgage, which were set artificially low and then reset. Many mortgages were packaged into securities sold to the public. Financial intermediaries (banks, thrifts, and mortgage companies) held the underlying mortgages only for a short period. Later, the same institutions sometimes bought some of the securities for their own portfolios.

Meanwhile, financial intermediaries borrowed short-term money in order to lend it longer-term. That practice exposes investors to the risk that they will not be able to refinance their borrowings, or will be able to do so only at higher interest rates. The interest rates on their securities remain fixed, resulting in losses for the financial intermediaries. The short-term borrowing to finance long-term lending was reminiscent of the first phase of the savings and loan (S&L) crisis of the 1980s. The subsequent bad loans on banks' books remind one of the second phase of the S&L crisis.

In sum, funding was at shorter and shorter maturities with interest rates heavily influenced by the Fed funds rate. Reportedly, some investment banks rolled over 25percent of their funding every night. That funding would have been extremely sensitive to changes in the Fed funds rate. Five year money came to be considered "long term" during the housing boom.

As a result, it became easier and easier for individuals to qualify for a residential mortgage. Down payments became smaller or even effectively disappeared. In turn, rating agencies apparently eased the requirements for what constituted a AAA mortgage-backed security.[4] Numerous public policy initiatives contributed to the easing of the terms of mortgages, and these policy initiatives fueled the rising home prices. These included various programs to make mortgages "affordable," thereby boosting demand. Meanwhile, other programs, such as "smart growth" policies, restricted the supply of housing. Easy credit stimulated the demand for housing, and smart growth policies restricted the supply. Together, these policies boosted housing prices to unsustainable levels.[5]

The boom phase ended when the Fed began raising interest rates. Housing prices first stopped rising in 2006 and then began declining. Mortgages started going into arrears, and homeowners walked away from their speculatively purchased homes. Many had no equity in their homes, and the fall in prices put them "underwater": their mortgage balance exceeded the value of their home.

As mortgage payments slowed, the value of mortgage-backed securities declined precipitously. That created the shock to the balance sheets of individuals and financial institutions. A balance sheet measures the assets and liabilities of individuals and firms. The difference (if positive) is their net worth or wealth position. The balance sheet shocks came first to heavily indebted homeowners caught up in the housing bubble; then to the institutions that financed the housing bubble directly or through their purchase of securities whose values were tied to mortgages; and finally to the general public whose savings were destroyed in the ensuing financial meltdown. Declining spending was a consequence of the balance sheet shock. The economy slid into recession (negative economic growth) at the end of 2008.

For banks, the balance sheet shocks led to capital impairment and diminished capacity to make fresh loans. On a bank's balance sheet, capital absorbs losses on loans and investments. When capital falls below safe levels, banks cannot afford to make new loans or buy fresh securities because they no longer have a cushion against future losses. Indeed, desired capital ratios are counter-cyclical, rising in economic downturns.

Regulatory Failure

Capital is vital for banks and other financial institutions. Capital is the difference in the value of the assets and liabilities of a bank. It is a cushion against losses on loans and investments, ensuring that banks can sustain some losses and yet remain viable. For regulated financial institutions like banks, capital ratios are set by law and regulation. In the crisis period, required capital ratios became doubly redundant. For impaired institutions, they simply could not be enforced. For those institutions that could raise capital, the desired capital ratio would exceed regulatory minimums. Markets compel the prudence in lending in down cycles that regulators dare not impose in booms.

Bad loans are made in good times, however, and it is in booms that prudent supervision over capital and lending standards is most needed. We know from history, however, that regulatory stringency is also counter-cyclical, declining in good times and rising in bad times. Financial services regulation has become dysfunctional, regardless of one's attitude towards government regulation in theory.

Even under a limited regulatory regime, the state is expected to provide protection against fraud. Yet every day there are fresh reports of fraud having occurred in the housing and mortgage markets. Thomas Ferguson and Robert Johnson examined the failure of regulators—especially the Fed—to deal with evident fraud in mortgage lending during the housing boom.[6] Even senior Federal Reserve officials acknowledge regulatory shortcomings. As Dallas Fed president Richard Fisher has said, "The regulators didn't do their job, including the Federal Reserve."[7]

The primary mission of bank regulatory agencies is to protect the safety and soundness of the banking system. These agencies include the Fed, the Office of the Comptroller of the Currency, the Federal Deposit Insurance Corporation, and state banking agencies.

The Securities and Exchange Commission oversees public companies generally and investment banks in particular. On the homepage of the Securities and Exchange Commission, a visitor can click on "What We Do" and be told the following: "The mission of the U.S. Securities and Exchange Commission is to protect investors, maintain fair, orderly, and efficient markets, and facilitate capital formation."[8] Along with the other financial services regulatory agencies, the SEC utterly failed in its stated mission. The Lehman failure, the forced mergers of Bear Stearns and Merrill Lynch, the failures and mergers of Wachovia and Washington Mutual, the AIG debacle, and the Madoff scandal are only the tip of the iceberg of regulatory failure.

This sorry record is one predicted by public choice theory: regulatory agencies are captured by the industries they regulate. Willem Buiter observes that "capture occurs when bureaucrats, regulators, judges or politicians, instead of serving the public interest as they are mandated to do, end up acting systematically to favor specific vested interests—often the very interests they were supposed to control or restrain in the public interest."[9]

To suppose the contrary would be to adopt what James Buchanan described as "a romantic and illusory theory" of politics, in which government officials selflessly act for the public good rather than for their own private interests.[10] Those advocating enhanced regulation in response to the current crisis must therefore explain why we should expect a reformed system to work any better in the future. Specifically, a regulatory system in the public interest must be designed to be incentive-compatible. The actual flesh-and-blood human beings doing the regulation must have an incentive to act in the public interest, rather than to capitulate to the demands of the regulated firms. That has not been true for financial services for a long time.

The bailouts of financial firms using taxpayer money speak loudly to the question of cui bono. The Treasury has announced that the nineteen largest financial firms will not be permitted to fail. It appears that taxpayer support of those firms has no limits. This is the very essence of crony capitalism: the use of public monies by government officials to the advantage of favored private interests. In such a system, profits are privatized, and losses are socialized. It is far from a free market. Capitalism without failure is like religion without sin. It doesn't work.

A great deal has been written about the failure of markets and capitalism in the current crisis. But the failure is at least as much one of government and government regulation. The financial system is one of the most highly regulated parts of the economy (as the extensive listing of regulatory agencies suggests). Yet the regulatory system failed in its mission of preserving the integrity of financial services firms and protecting the consumer.

Diagnosing the Crisis

The housing boom was a classic credit induced bubble: an unsustainable rise in asset prices. It exemplified the bubbles already familiar to economists by the nineteenth century. Economists developed an analysis of these booms and busts that came to be known as business cycle theory. Joseph Schumpeter noted the "pivotal importance" of the fact that "constructional" (construction-related) industries exhibit relatively greater volatility over business cycles than producers of consumer goods. Public figures have repeatedly spoken of the "unprecedented" nature of the current crisis, but the volatility of capital goods, and especially "constructional" industries, was already a commonplace among economists by the end of the nineteenth century.[11]

The prices of long-lived capital are especially sensitive to changes in the real (inflation-adjusted) rate of interest. The value of future events—income, benefits, or costs—is smaller than that of present events. The future is discounted by interest rates to a present value. The future flows of income or other valuable services (such as housing services) become more valuable as interest rates fall. The lower the rate, the lower the discount for future events.

The prices of long-lived capital, including housing, thus tend to rise in eras of low real interest rates. (The reverse is also true.) As we have seen, there was a sustained period of historically low interest rates for a crucial three-year period that fueled the housing boom and a corresponding stock market bubble.

Fearing the onset of price inflation, the Fed began raising the Fed funds rate in June 2004. At their December 2004 meeting, the Federal Open Market Committee (FOMC) raised the target for the Fed funds rate to 2.25 percent. That was the first time the rate had topped 2 percent since the October 2001 meeting. In a series of steps, the FOMC continued raising the target until it peaked at 5.25 percent at the June 2006 meeting. Thus, in the course of two years, the FOMC had raised the Fed funds rate from 1 percent to 5.25 percent. Not surprisingly, the housing bubble then burst, and a financial crisis ensued.

The current crisis is both a classic financial crisis and a deep recession. There has been a panic quality to the crisis. There have been runs on bank deposits and runs on the commercial paper of some issuers. I have emphasized the balance sheet aspects of the crisis because policymakers have systematically misidentified the problem as one of liquidity.

Liquidity and Capital Impairment

Liquidity is a term of art signifying ready funds that can be quickly spent. Cash and cash equivalents, such as short-term securities of high quality, are the most liquid assets. Individuals and corporations in some cases found themselves illiquid. The ability to borrow at reasonable interest rates can be a substitute for liquid assets. That ability depends, of course, on others' having liquid assets to lend.

In the current crisis there have been liquidity "events," as in the drying up of finance through commercial paper for Lehman that led to that bank's quick collapse. Other commercial paper issuers have had less life-threatening periods of difficulty raising short-term funds. Since deposit insurance limits were raised to $250,000 per insured account, banks have had no reported difficulties funding themselves through deposits. It is now the creditworthiness of the federal government, not that of the individual bank, that matters. Thus far the government's creditworthiness has held up.

If markets doubt the value of assets on an institution's books, they will either not supply funds or do so for shorter and shorter durations and at higher and higher interest rates. Capital impairment is the real culprit in the crisis, but policymakers have perceived it to be a liquidity problem. Only additional capital, not more liquidity, can resolve the problem. That is why the TARP, as originally conceived, was misguided. It was aimed at providing liquidity, not capital. And this is also why all the Fed's credit programs to date have had limited success, at best.

Government provision of capital to banks, as occurred in the Depression era Reconstruction Finance Corporation, could, in principle, have helped. The actual provision of capital to banks by the Bush and Obama administrations did not follow the RFC model and was bungled. Institutions should have been "stress-tested" before receiving capital injections, not after. Failing that, there was no way to determine how much capital the banks actually needed. There was no determination of which banks were hopelessly under-capitalized and needed to be closed.

The multiple injections of government money into the same institutions (as with Citigroup and Bank of America) are evidence that insufficient funds were provided initially. Whether the new requirements for some banks to raise fresh capital will suffice depends on whether the Treasury's stress-testing of banks was severe enough. On that, there is conflicting evidence.[12]

Fed chairman Ben Bernanke reminds us that he studied the Great Depression of the 1930s, but he evidently learned the wrong lessons. Providing liquidity is a tonic for a squeeze in short-term credit markets. The Depression began with that problem, and its severity would have been mitigated by providing liquidity (i.e., by monetary expansion rather than contraction). That was the correct lesson.

But in the case of the Great Depression there was monetary contraction and an economic downturn that turned into a depression. Then there was a series of banking panics. The banking system was stabilized not by Fed action, but by the eventual recapitalization of the remaining institutions. That is where the RFC played a role by providing capital to banks and other firms. Capital-starved institutions need capital, not loans. In fact, the RFC started as a lending program and was unsuccessful until it was converted into a capital provider.[13]

I am not suggesting by any means that public provision of capital is to be preferred over private provision. I am arguing, however, that the public-policy response to the current crisis has generally been ill-conceived and has failed to learn from historical experience in our own country. Again, the public policy of both the Bush and Obama administrations appears to have been more focused on protecting particular private interests rather than the public interest.

For the most part, the Fed has been doing two things. First, through its many special credit facilities, it has been conducting fiscal policy through credit allocation. Second, it has provided massive injections of liquidity to financial markets ("open-market" operations). These liquidity injections have done little to relieve the holes in the banks' balance sheets, but they have created the potential for inflation down the road.

Easy credit and regulatory forbearance fueled the housing boom. Easy credit and regulatory forbearance is not the solution to the bust. The recession and financial crisis in which we still find ourselves is the result of a credit-induced housing boom, which, in turn, fueled a consumption bubble. Households and firms were left over indebted. The solution to that is a restoration of balance sheets across the economy through higher savings rates.

By consuming a lower proportion of income for a time, individuals and families accumulate funds to replenish their lost wealth. Additionally, the crisis has provided a valuable lesson: households need savings to weather financial storms. Houses are not liquid assets, and a home is not an ATM machine. Having equity in a house is not a substitute for having money in the bank.

It would not be surprising to see the personal savings rate rebound from near zero to a more traditional level of 6 to 8 percent of personal income. As this is being written, it appears that consumers are in the process of making that adjustment.[14] The recent very low savings rate was a byproduct of the housing bubble and should vanish with it.[15]

Consumers and businesses are attempting to save more but are being frustrated by public policy. Almost everything the Treasury and Fed have done is designed to stimulate spending through debt creation, while more savings and further debt reduction are the needed remedies. This is what is known as de-leveraging. Additionally, the U.S. deficits and accumulating debt threaten America's future.[16]

If the government wanted to do something constructive, it should have permanently reduced taxes by cutting marginal tax rates. Only permanent tax cuts provide substantial and enduring benefits. Temporary tax cuts have only a fleeting and comparatively small effect on the economy. John Taylor examined the specific case of the Economic Stimulus Act of 2008 (passed in February of that year), which sent rebate checks totaling $100 billion to individuals and families. He concluded that "the rebates caused no statistically signify cant increase in consumption."[17]

Lawrence Lindsey proposed instead a permanent halving of the payroll tax. He estimated the direct revenue effects at $400 billion. The cut would have an immediate impact on households—with the very first paycheck—and help households restore their balance sheets. By lowering labor costs, the policy would encourage hiring. There are plenty of bold tax cuts with immediate, positive effects that could have been implemented.[18]

Government programs to prop up home prices have been half-hearted and ineffective overall, and mercifully so. Falling home prices are not the problem, but the solution, to the housing bust. In the bursting of an asset bubble, prices can go into what can appear to be a free fall.

What eventually stops the fall is that, at some point, asset prices decline so much that speculators are tempted by the prospect of abnormally high future rates of return from holding the asset. In the case of housing, that includes, importantly, first-time home buyers. The decline in home prices can clear the market in less time than normal home-buying would take to work off excess inventories of homes. If markets are left to operate freely, then the speculative forces that contributed to the boom can help halt the bust. A recent report chronicled the market forces at work in the Phoenix real estate market. A 50 percent drop in home prices there has attracted speculative buyers from as far away as Canada.[19] Anecdotal evidence and some sales data suggest that the process is also at work in various local real estate markets, including the Bay Area and Reno, Nevada.

Some analysts have argued that allowing asset markets to clear will result in the "undershooting" of prices. Prices will fall more than necessary, causing needless losses. That argument misconstrues the purposes of markets and the capabilities of pricing models. We lack the information to know when prices are "undershooting." It is only by actual transactions that price movements produce the information that investors use to make calculations of expected profits. Only when the successful entrepreneurs book extraordinary profits do we know—after the fact—that most investors were overlooking profitable opportunities. Those analysts who are sure markets have mispriced homes should put some skin in the game and start buying.

To end an asset bust, there is no alternative to allowing prices for the asset to decline to the point that new buyers are attracted into the market for those assets. That is true whether we are talking about housing markets, which are localized, or global securities markets.

The Way Forward

In the current crisis we have had repeated misdiagnoses of the nature of the problem and poorly prescribed remedies. The actual economic problems have gone un- treated and correct treatments thwarted. The policy responses of the Bush/Obama regimes are as far off the mark as many of those implemented in the Hoover/Roosevelt Great Depression.

The way forward must include reliance on the innovative spirit of Americans and the resilience of their economy. Government can implement good policies but, in the absence of that, "do no harm" must be the guiding principle. A great deal of harm has already been done by the response of the Bush and Obama administrations.

President Obama's advisers claim to be following the policy prescriptions of Keynesian economics: spend and run deficits. That response is particularly ill suited to the current crisis. The current crisis is at root not one of an aggregate demand failure, but a balance-sheet shock brought on by a credit-induced housing boom and subsequent bust.[20] The housing boom was financed by a complex array of securities and other financial products. In many cases, the financial products were poorly designed.[21] In any case, their value was severely compromised when the housing boom ended, i.e., once housing prices stopped rising.

Financial stability and economic growth will come again after the bursting of the asset bubble has run its course, savings have increased, and balance sheets have been restored. Easy credit and stimulus to consumption (for which most government spending is designed) are counter-productive for the adjustment process. Moreover, easy credit risks inflating another bubble.

Gerald P. O'Driscoll Jr. is a senior fellow at the Cato Institute and was formerly vice president at the Federal Reserve Bank of Dallas and later at Citigroup. With Mario J. Rizzo, he is co-author of The Economics of Time and Ignorance (1996).

SOURCES

1. Brian M. Carney, "Bernanke Is Fighting the Last War," interview with Anna Schwartz, Wall Street Journal, and October 18–19, 2008.

2. John B. Taylor, Getting Off Track: How Government Actions and Interventions Caused, Prolonged, and Worsened the Financial Crisis (Palo Alto, CA: Hoover Institution Press, 2009), 1–11.

3. For the historical series, go to:
    http://www.bankofengland.co.uk/statistics/rates/baserate.pdf.

4. Gary Gorton, "The Panic of 2007," National Bureau of Economic Research Working Paper, no. 14358. Available at: http://www.nber.org/papers/w14358.

5. Thomas Sowell, The Housing Boom and Bust (New York: Basic Books, 2009).

6. Thomas Ferguson and Robert Johnson, "Too Big to Fail: The 'Paulson Put,' Presidential Politics, and the Global Financial Meltdown, Part 1: From Shadow Financial System to Shadow Bailout," International Journal of Political Economy38 (Spring 2009): 3–34.

7. Mary Anastasia O'Grady, "Don't Monetize the Debt," interview with Richard Fisher, Wall Street Journal, May 23–24, 2009.

8. www.sec.org

9. Willem H. Buiter, "Central Banks and Financial Crises," paper presented at the Federal Reserve Bank of Kansas City symposium on "Maintaining Stability in a Changing Financial System" in Jackson Hole, WY, August 21–23, 2008.

10. James M. Buchanan, "Politics without Romance: A Sketch of Public Choice Theory and Its Normative Implications," in The Collected Works of James M. Buchanan, Vol. I: The Logical Foundations of Constitutional Liberty (Indianapolis: Liberty Fund, 2003), 46.

11. Joseph A. Schumpeter, History of Economic Analysis (Oxford: Oxford University Press, 1954), 1126 and 1126n8.

12. Ken Beauchemin and Brent Meyer, "How Realistic Were the Economic Forecasts Used in the Stress Tests?" Economic Trends, Federal Reserve Bank of Cleveland (May 2009): 28–30. Available at: http://www.clevelandfed.org/research/trends/2009/0509/ET_may09.pdf

13. Walker Todd, "History and Rationales for the Reconstruction Finance Corporation," Quarterly Review of the Cleveland Federal Reserve Bank28, no. 1 (Quarter 1, 1992): 22–35. Available at: http://www.clevelandfed.org/research/review/1992/92-q4-todd.pdf.

14. Kelly Evans, "Americans Save More, Amid Rising Confidence," Wall Street Journal, June 27–28, 2009.

15. The personal savings rate from 1959 to early 2009 can be found at http://research.stlouisfed.org/fred2/data/PSAVERT.txt

16. John Taylor, "Exploding debt threatens America," Financial Times, May 26, 2009.

17. Taylor, Getting Off Track, 21.

18. Lawrence Lindsey, "Not All Stimuli Are Created Equal," Weekly Standard, January 5, 2009.

19. David Streitfeld, "Amid Housing Bust, Phoenix Begins a New Frenzy," New York Times, May 24, 2009. Available at: http://www.nytimes.com/2009/05/24/business/24phoenix.html?_r=28th&emc=th

20. Axel Leijonhufvud, "Wicksell, Hayek, Keynes, Friedman: Whom Should We Follow?" paper presented at the Special Meeting of the Mont Pelérin Society, "The End of Globalizing Capitalism? Classical Liberal Responses to the Global Financial Crisis," New York City, March 5–7, 2009.

21. Gorton, "The Panic of 2007."

CHAPTER SIX

DIABETES - STATE LEGISLATION OVERVIEW

National Conference of State Legislatures
October 2009

Approximately 24 million Americans have been diagnosed with diabetes, about 8 percent of the US population. It is the eighth leading cause of death in the United States and can lead to painful and costly health complications including nervous system damage, heart disease, stroke, blindness, and kidney disease. According to the Centers for Disease Control and Prevention (CDC), in 2007, the medical costs associated with diabetes were $116 billion and the indirect costs (disability, work loss, premature mortality) were $58 billion. State legislatures throughout the country are actively exploring policy options to deal with this growing problem.

Many state legislatures considered diabetes related legislation in the 2007, 2008 and 2009 sessions. The introduced legislation mainly focused on the areas of research, public education, diabetes prevention and management. Below are a number of tables that provide examples of various diabetes legislative options enacted in 2007, 2008 and 2009.

Summary of 2007-2009 Diabetes Legislation

Diabetes Month or Day

In 2007 and 2008 three states designated a day or month recognizing the disease of diabetes. Six states enacted diabetes day or month legislation in 2009. By doing this, legislatures can increase public awareness about the disease, as well as encourage public education and prevention measures.

State /Bill#	Title and Description (blue shading indicates enacted measures)
Colorado SJR 27 (Adopted- 2009)	American Diabetes Alert Day: Proclaims March 14, 2009 as American Diabetes Alert Day.
Kansas HR 6021 (Adopted- 2009)	Diabetes Alert Day: Recognized March 24, 2009 as American Diabetes Alert Day in Kansas.
Michigan HR 136 (Adopted- 2007)	Juvenile Diabetes Awareness: Recognizes June 17-23, 2007, as Juvenile Diabetes Awareness Week.
Michigan HR 226 (Adopted- 2007)	Diabetes Awareness Month: Recognizes November 2007 as Diabetes Awareness Month.
Michigan HR 327 (Adopted- 2007)	Kidney Disease: Observes April 16, 2008, as Michigan Kidney Disease and Diabetes Awareness Day.
Mississippi SCR 654 (Adopted- 2009)	Diabetes Discovery Week: Relates to designate Diabetes Discovery Week in Mississippi.
New Jersey HR 86 (Adopted- 2008)	American Diabetes Month: Recognizes November 2008 as American Diabetes Month.
Nevada SCR 20 (Adopted- 2009)	Diabetes Awareness Day: Designates March 25, 2009 as Diabetes Awareness Day in Nevada.
Pennsylvania HR 495 (Adopted- 2007)	Diabetes Month: Recognizes November 2007 as National Diabetes Month.
Texas HR 350 (Adopted- 2009)	Diabetes Day: Recognizes March 17, 2009 as Diabetes Day at the State Capital.

Disparities

Minority populations are affected by diabetes at a much higher rate than the rest of the population. For example, African Americans and Hispanics/Latinos are twice as likely to have diabetes. An African American or Hispanic/Latino born in the US in 2000 has a 2 in 5 risk for developing diabetes. Reducing and eliminating these disparities are important public health goals. Three states enacted legislation related to diabetes disparities in 2007 and 2008.

State /Bill#	Title and Description (blue shading indicates enacted measures)
Illinois S 654 (Enacted- 2007) ILC § 4055/5	Diabetes Initiative Act: Creates the Illinois State Diabetes Commission to look at ways to slow the rate of diabetes, prevention and disparities through 2010.
Illinois S 776 (Enacted- 2007) ILC § 135/10-32	Condition of African American Men: Creates the Task Force on the Condition of African American Men to reduce diabetes disparities. The purposes of the Task Force are to: determine the causal factors for the condition of African American men; to inventory State programs and initiatives that serve to improve the condition of African American men; to identify gaps in services to African American men; and to develop strategies to reduce duplication of services and to maximize coordination between State agencies, providers, and educational institutions, including developing benchmarks to measure progress.
Massachusetts S 2426 (Enacted- 2007) MGL 6A § 16O(a)	Health Care Access: Provides for a health disparities council within the executive office of health and human services to eliminate disparities in health care related to breast, cervical, prostate and colorectal cancers, strokes, heat attacks, diabetes, infant mortality, lupus, HIV/AIDS, asthma and other respiratory diseases.

| Michigan HR 514 (Adopted- 2007) | Department of Community Health: Urges Department of Community Health to take further actions to address disparities by completing the development of a long range strategic plan to reduce health disparities and seek to partner with county health departments, community groups, minority health coalitions and private sector entities on the development of interventions and an appropriate health promotion and disease management program. |

Prevention

Prevention of diabetes includes both preventing the onset of diabetes, as well as preventing serious health complications once someone is diagnosed with diabetes. Maintaining a healthy weight, getting regular exercise, eating nutritiously, getting regular medical check-ups, and communicating with one's physician are all important steps an individual can take to reduce the risk of diabetes. Studies show that people at high risk for type 2 diabetes can prevent or delay the onset of the disease by losing 5 to 7 percent of their body weight. A person that has already been diagnosed with diabetes can prevent and/or delay diabetes-related health complications by managing their diabetes through testing, regular medical check-ups, appropriate treatment and eating a diet appropriate for people with diabetes. Legislatures in six states examined policy options aimed at diabetes prevention and management in 2007 and 2007. In 2009, six states enacted diabetes prevention and management legislation.

State /Bill#	Title and Description (blue shading indicates enacted measures)
Georgia H 228 (Enacted- 2009) OCGA § 31-2-17	State Health and Human Services Agencies: Requires the appointment of a diabetes coordinator to work with other state departments to ensure all diabetes related programs are coordinated.
Illinois S 654 (Enacted- 2007) ILC §4055/5	Diabetes Initiative Act: Requires that the Department of Health Services shall develop a strategic plan to slow the rate of diabetes by the year 2010. The will identify barriers to effective screening compliance and treatment for diabetes, identify methods to increase the number of beneficiaries who will screen regularly for diabetes, review current medical therapies and best clinical practices for diabetes, and identify actions to be taken to reduce the morbidity and mortality from diabetes by the year 2010 and a time line for taking those actions.
Illinois S 2012 (Enacted- 2007) ILC § 2310/2310-76	Department of Public Health Powers: Establishes a Task Force on Chronic Disease Prevention and Health Promotion to study and make recommendations regarding the structure of the chronic disease prevention and health promotion system in Illinois, as well as changes that should be made to the system. On or before July 1, 2010, the Task force shall make recommendations to the Director of Public Health on reforming the delivery system for chronic disease prevention and health promotion, ensuring adequate funding for infrastructure and delivery of programs, addressing health disparity, and the role of health promotion and chronic disease prevention in support of State spending on health care.

Iowa H 478 (Enacted- 2009) IC § 514C.18	Health Insurance Coverage: Requires health insurance coverage for diabetes self management training and education programs. Provides that diabetes education programs must cover a certain number of hours of initial outpatient diabetes self-management training within a continuous twelve-month period and up to two hours of follow up training for each subsequent year for an individual diagnosed by a physician with any type of diabetes.
Mississippi H 1530 (Enacted- 2009) Chapter 435	Obesity: Creates a pilot program to reduce obesity and diabetes in the state through education and disease management.
New Jersey A 2932 (Pending- 2008; Assembly State Government Committee)	Vending Machines: Would require at least 30% of snacks sold in State vending machines be appropriate for consumption by individuals with diabetes.
New Jersey A 1711 (Pending- 2008; Senate Transportation Committee)	Special License Plates: Would establish special license plates to fund diabetes education, prevention and research. Monies collected from all fees for diabetes research and awareness license plates will be deposited into a non-lapsing, interest-bearing Diabetes Research and Awareness Fund for diabetes education, prevention, and research projects.
New Jersey S 1891 (Pending- 2008; Senate Transportation Committee)	Juvenile Diabetes License Plates: Would establish special license plates to fund juvenile diabetes research and education. Would create the Juvenile Diabetes License Plate Fund to fund American Diabetes Association and Juvenile Diabetes Research Foundation for education, prevention and research projects in New Jersey.
New Mexico HJM 24 (Enacted- 2009)	Chronic Disease in the Work Force: Requires a study of the cost and impact of chronic disease, including diabetes, on workforce and business-based wellness programs.

New York S 2104 (Enacted- 2007) Chapter 54	Health and Mental Hygiene Budget: Appropriates $ 600,000 to the New York state Diabetes Prevention and Control program
Ohio H 119 (Enacted- 2007) OHC § 293.10	Appropriations for Operation of State Programs: Appropriates $500,000 to the Healthy Ohio program to support evidence-based programs for diabetes prevention and management, utilizing proven behavior change strategies. The program will also provide screening for diabetes, and those with a high risk of diabetes will get education on diabetes, diabetes management, physical activity and eating habits, and opportunities for monitored physical activity for adults and families.
Oregon H 2009 (Enacted- 2009) ORS § 587.2	State Health Authority: Oregon Health Authority shall develop, by the year 2009, a strategic plan to start to slow the rate of diabetes caused by obesity and other environmental factors by the year 2010. Plan to include: (a) Identification of environmental factors that encourage or support physical activity and healthy eating habits; (b) Identification of preventative strategies that are effective and culturally competent and that meet the populations most at risk for developing diabetes; (c) Recommendations for evidence-based screening; (d) Recommendations for redesigning and financing primary care practices that would facilitate adoption of the Chronic Care Model for screening for diabetes, support for patient self-management and regular reporting of preventative clinical screening results and; (e) Identification of actions to be taken to reduce the morbidity and mortality from diabetes by the year 2015 and a time frame for taking those actions.

	Early Diabetic Screening and Treatment:
Pennsylvania HR 386 (Enacted- 2007)	Encourages individuals to seek early screening and early treatment of diabetic conditions and encourages health care providers to improve care to better control diabetes.
Tennessee H 2270 (Enacted- 2009) T.C. § 4-40-403(c)	Diabetes Health Care Grants: Makes all schools eligible for grants from the Tennessee Center for Diabetes Prevention and Health Improvement.
Texas H 1990 (Enacted- 2009) TAC § 531.0319	Diabetes Self Management Pilot Program: Creates a diabetes self-management training pilot program for State Medicaid participants.
Virginia H 29 (Enacted- 2008) Chapter 847	Budget Bill: Appropriates $5,000 to the Russell County Health Department for a diabetic outreach program.
Virginia H 30 (Enacted- 2008) Chapter 879	Budget Bill: Appropriates $196,263 in support of diabetes prevention, education, and public service at the Virginia Center for Diabetes Professional Education at the University of Virginia.

Reporting of Self-Identification

Requiring reports as to the number of people with diabetes in a given region creates a data set that can be a powerful tool. It can allow state diabetes programs to focus their resources in the areas where diabetes is most prevalent. It is important to know how many people have diabetes, where they are, and who cares for them. This information can help in assessing how state programs are doing in preventing and controlling diabetes and determining where future resources would be most useful. Self-identification of people with diabetes on a driver's license or other state-issued identification can facilitate emergency medical treatment. Three states looked at diabetes legislation relating to reporting or self-identification in 2007-2008 and three states enacted reporting or self-identification legislation in 2009.

State / Bill #	Title and Description (blue shading indicates enacted measures
Illinois H 2481 (Enacted- 2009) ILCS § 2310-640	Department of Public Health Powers and Duties Law: Requires the development and implementation of a neonatal diabetes mellitus registry to track glycosylated hemoglobin levels.
New Jersey A 1711 (Pending- 2008; Assembly Transportation, Public Works and Independent Authorities Committee) and S 1182 (Pending- 2008; Senate Transportation Committee)	Special Diabetes License Plates: Would establish special license plates to fund diabetes education, prevention and research. Monies collected from all fees for diabetes research and awareness license plates would be deposited into a non-lapsing, interest-bearing Diabetes Research and Awareness Fund for diabetes education, prevention, and research project.
South Dakota H 1202 (Enacted- 2009) SDS §32-12A-24	School Bus Drivers Licenses: Allows persons with insulin-treated diabetes mellitus to get an endorsement on their commercial driver license.
Texas H 1363 (Enacted- 2009) Chapter 706(c)	Diabetes Mellitus Registry: Creates a statewide voluntary diabetes registry.
Virginia H 1299 (Enacted- 2008) Code of VA § 46.2-342	Revised Uniform Anatomical Gift Act: Puts identification for insulin dependent diabetics on their drivers license.
District of Columbia B 148 (Enacted- 2007) Law 20 § 5069	Fiscal Year 2008 Budget Support Act of 2007: requires the Department of Health to provide a comprehensive diabetes report annually.

Research

Funding and promoting diabetes research is essential if innovations in prevention, testing, management, and possibly even a cure are to come about. States have been active in promoting and conducting diabetes research during the 2007 and 2008 sessions. Seven states explored their options related to diabetes research legislation in 2007-2008 and three states enacted legislation in 2009.

State /Bill #	Title and Description (blue shading indicates enacted measures)
Illinois H 5701 (Enacted- 2007)	FY09 Appropriations: Appropriates $100,000 for diabetes research, payable from the Diabetes Research Check-off Fund.
Florida S 1840 (Enacted- 2009) FLS § 210.011	Health Care: Allocates monies collected from cigarette taxes to the Diabetes Research Institute.
Michigan H 4344 (Enacted- 2007) Public Act 123	Department of Community Health Appropriations: Appropriates $3,999,500 to the Diabetes and Kidney Program for research, prevention, and public education.
Michigan H 4493 and S 436 (enacted- 2007) Public Act 41	Supplemental Appropriations: Appropriates $25,000 to the Morris Hood State University for diabetes research.
New Mexico HJM 24 (Adopted- 2009)	Chronic Disease in the Work Force: Requests the Health Department do a study on the cost and impact of chronic disease, including diabetes, on workforce and business-based wellness programs.
New Jersey A 669 (Pending-2008; Assembly Health and Senior Services Committee) and S 1681 (Pending- 2008; Senate Health, Human Services and Senior Citizens Committee)	Embryonic Stem Cell Research: Would prohibit use of public funds for embryonic stem cell research.

New Jersey A
1711 (Pending-
2008; Assembly
Transportation,
Public Works and
Independent Authorities
Committee) and S
1182 (Pending- 2008;
Senate Transportation
Committee)

Special Diabetes License Plates: Would
establish special license plates to fund diabetes
education, prevention and research. Monies
collected from all fees for diabetes research and
awareness license plates would be deposited
into a non-lapsing, interest-bearing Diabetes
Research and Awareness Fund for diabetes
education, prevention, and research projects.

New Jersey S 1891
(Pending- 2008;
Senate Transportation
Committee

Juvenile Diabetes License Plates: Would
establish special license plates to fund juvenile
diabetes research and education.

Oregon H 2009
(Enacted- 2009) ORS §
587.2

State Health Authority: Oregon Health
Authority shall develop, by the year 2009,
a strategic plan to start to slow the rate
of diabetes caused by obesity and other
environmental factors by the year 2010. Plan
to include (a) Identification of environmental
factors that encourage or support physical
activity and healthy eating habits; (b)
Identification of preventative strategies that
are effective and culturally competent and
that meet the populations most at risk for
developing diabetes; (c) Recommendations
for evidence-based screening; (d)
Recommendations for redesigning and
financing primary care practices that would
facilitate adoption of the Chronic Care Model
for screening for diabetes, support for patient
self-management and regular reporting of
preventative clinical screening results and; (e)
Identification of actions to be taken to reduce
the morbidity and mortality from diabetes
by the year 2015 and a time frame for taking
those actions.

Pennsylvania H 1589 (Enacted- 2007) Act 2008-41	Capital Budget: Appropriates $20,000,000 to the University of Pittsburgh Medical Center/ University of Pittsburgh Diabetes Institute.
Rhode Island H 5672 (Adopted- 2007)	Study Commission Creation: Creates a nine member special legislative study commission to do a comprehensive study of the potential for and barriers to the advancement of regenerative medicine and related research.

Tax Related

States looked at tax related diabetes legislation in two policy areas. Some proposed bills would create an income tax check-off box for taxpayer gifts to diabetes research, education, prevention and management. This allows for additional funds to be raised for diabetes programs without raising taxes or taking away funds from other programs. Other proposed bills would provide for an exemption for diabetes medical supplies from sales and use tax. During the 2007 and 2008 legislative sessions, eight states looked at tax related diabetes legislation. While none of the bills were enacted, they are included in this legislative report to highlight the upcoming trend in tax related diabetes legislation.

State / Bill #	Title and Description (blue shading indicates enacted measures)
Illinois H 3409 (Did not pass- 2007)	Juvenile Diabetes Research Donation: Would provide that an applicant for a driver's license or instruction permit, a commercial driver's license or instruction permit, or a State identification card shall be asked if he or she wants to donate $1 to the Juvenile Diabetes Research and Nutritional Health Trust Fund. Would create the Juvenile Diabetes Research and Nutritional Health Trust Fund and provide that all moneys in the Fund shall be used by the Department of Public Health for juvenile diabetes research, nutritional health programs, education, and public awareness.

Massachusetts H 2842 and S 1811 (Did not pass- 2007)	Exemption of Sales Taxes for Certain Medical Devices: Would provide for an exemption from the sales tax for diabetes monitoring and testing supplies.
New Jersey S 1418 (Pending- 2008; Senate Budget and Appropriations Committee)	Multi-State Streamlined Sales Tax Agreement: Would provide for an exemption for diabetic supplies from taxes under "Sales and Use Tax Act"
New York A 2408 and S 1275 (Did not pass- 2007)	Corporate Franchise Tax Check-off: Would provide for a corporate franchise tax check-off and a personal income tax check-off for taxpayer gifts for diabetes research and education; would establish the diabetes research and education fun
Ohio H 368 (Did not pass- 2007)	Tangible Personal Property Sales and Use Tax Exemption: Would provide for an exemption of diabetic supplies from the sales and use tax.
Ohio S 75 (Did not pass- 2007)	Income Tax Return Contributions: Would allow taxpayers to contribute to the American Diabetes Association through their income tax return
Pennsylvania H 1834 and S 90 (Did not pass- 2007)	Tax Reform Code: Would provide for charitable check-offs by taxpayers to the Juvenile Diabetes Cure Research Fund.
Rhode Island S 606 and S 2571 (Did not pass- 2007)	Taxation: Would exempt from sales taxes diabetic monitoring kits, including, but not limited to, testing strips utilized for the determination of blood sugar levels
Virginia H 1592 (Did not pass- 2007)	Retail Sales and Use Tax: Would exempt diabetic supplies from retail sale and use tax.

CHAPTER SEVEN

SUMMARY REPORT

OF THE

REVIEW OF U.S. HUMAN SPACE FLIGHT PLANS COMMITTEE

The U.S. human spaceflight program appears to be on an unsustainable trajectory. It is perpetuating the perilous practice of pursuing goals that do not match allocated resources. Space operations are among the most complex and unforgiving pursuits ever undertaken by humans. It really is rocket science. Space operations become all the more difficult when means do not match aspirations. Such is the case today.

The nation is facing important decisions on the future of human spaceflight. Will we leave the close proximity of low-Earth orbit, where astronauts have circled since 1972, and explore the solar system, charting a path for the eventual expansion of human civilization into space? If so, how will we ensure that our exploration delivers the greatest benefit to the nation? Can we explore with reasonable assurances of human safety? And, can the nation marshal the resources to embark on the mission?

Whatever space program is ultimately selected, it must be matched with the resources needed for its execution. How can we marshal the necessary resources? There are actually more options available today than in 1961 when President Kennedy challenged NASA and the nation to "land a man on the Moon by the end of the decade."

First, space exploration has become a global enterprise. Many nations have aspirations in space, and the combined annual budgets of their space programs are comparable to NASA's. If the United States is willing to lead a global program of exploration, sharing both the burden and benefit of space exploration in a meaningful way, significant benefits could follow. Actively engaging international partners in a manner adapted to today's multi-polar world could strengthen geopolitical relationships, leverage global resources, and enhance the exploration enterprise.

Second, there is now a burgeoning commercial space industry. If we craft the space architecture to provide opportunities to this industry, there is the potential—not without risk—that the costs to the government would be reduced. Finally, we are also more experienced than in 1961, and able to build on that experience as we design an exploration program. If, after designing cleverly, building alliances with partners, and engaging commercial providers, the nation cannot afford to fund the effort to pursue the goals it would like to embrace, it should accept the disappointment of setting lesser goals.

Can we explore with reasonable assurances of human safety? Human space travel has many benefits, but it is an inherently dangerous endeavor. Human safety can never be absolutely assured, but throughout this report, it is treated as a sine qua non. It is not discussed in extensive detail because any concepts falling short in human safety have simply been eliminated from consideration.

How will we explore to deliver the greatest benefit to the nation? Planning for a human spaceflight program should begin with a choice about its goals—rather than a choice of possible destinations. Destinations should derive from goals, and alternative architectures may be weighed against those goals. There is now a strong consensus in the United States that the next step in human spaceflight is to travel beyond low-Earth orbit. This should carry important benefits to society, including: driving technological innovation; developing commercial industries and important national capabilities; and contributing to our expertise in further exploration. Human exploration can contribute appropriately to the expansion of scientific knowledge, particularly in areas such as field geology, and it is in the interest of both science and human spaceflight that a credible and well-rationalized strategy of coordination between them be developed. Crucially, human spaceflight objectives should broadly align with key national objectives.

These more tangible benefits exist within a larger context. Exploration provides an opportunity to demonstrate space leadership while deeply engaging international partners; to inspire the next generation of scientists and engineers; and to shape human perceptions of our place in the universe.

The Committee concluded that the ultimate goal of human exploration is to chart a path for human expansion into the solar system. This is an ambitious goal, but one worthy of U.S. leadership in concert with a broad range of international partners.

The Committee's task was to review the U.S. plans for human spaceflight. In doing so, it assessed the programs within the current human spaceflight portfolio; considered capabilities and technologies a future program might require; and considered the roles of commercial industry and our international partners in this enterprise. From these deliberations, the Committee developed five integrated alternatives for the U.S. human spaceflight program. The considerations and the five alternatives are summarized in the pages that follow.

Key Questions to Guide the Plan for Human Spaceflight

The Committee identified the following questions that, if answered, would form the basis of a plan for U.S. human spaceflight:

1. What should be the future of the Space Shuttle?
2. What should be the future of the International Space Station (ISS)?
3. On what should the next heavy-lift launch vehicle be based?
4. How should crews be carried to low-Earth orbit?
5. What is the most practicable strategy for exploration beyond low-Earth orbit?

The Committee considers the framing and answering of these questions individually, and in a consistent way, to be at least as important as their combinations in the integrated options for a human spaceflight program.

1.0 CURRENT PROGRAMS

Before addressing options for the future human exploration program, it is appropriate to discuss the current programs: the Space Shuttle, ISS and Constellation, as well as the looming problem of "the Gap."

1.1. Space Shuttle

What should be the future of the Space Shuttle? The present plan is to retire it at the end of FY 2010, with its final flight scheduled for the last month of that fiscal year. Although the current

Administration has relaxed the requirement to complete the last mission before the end of FY 2010, there are no funds in the FY 2011 budget for continuing Shuttle operations.

In considering the future of the Shuttle, the Committee assessed the realism of the current schedule; examined issues related to Shuttle workforce, reliability and cost; and weighed the risks and possible benefits of a Shuttle extension. The Committee noted that the projected flight rate is nearly twice that of the actual flight rate since return to flight after the Columbia accident. Recognizing that undue schedule and budget pressure can subtly impose a negative influence on safety, the Committee finds that a more realistic schedule is prudent. With the remaining flights likely to stretch into the second quarter of 2011, the Committee considers it important to budget for Shuttle operations through that time.

Although a thorough analysis of Shuttle safety was not part of its charter, the Committee did examine the Shuttle's safety record and reliability. New human-rated launch vehicles will likely be more reliable once they reach maturity, but in the meantime, the Shuttle is in the enviable position of being through its infant mortality phase. Its flight experience and demonstrated reliability should not be discounted.

Once the Shuttle is retired, there will be a gap in America's capability to launch humans into space. That gap will extend until the next U.S. human-rated launch system becomes available. The Committee estimates that, under the current plan, this gap will be at least seven years long. There has not been this long a gap in U.S. human launch capability since the U.S. human space program began.

Most of the integrated options presented below would retire the Shuttle after a prudent flyout of the current manifest, indicating that the Committee found the interim reliance on international crew services acceptable. However, one option does provide for an extension of Shuttle at a minimum safe flight rate to preserve U.S. capability to launch astronauts into space. If that option is selected, there should be a thorough review of Shuttle recertification conducted to date and overall Shuttle reliability to ensure that the risk associated with that extension would be acceptable. This review should be performed by an independent committee, with the purpose to ensure that NASA has met the intent behind the relevant recommendation of the Columbia Accident Investigation Board[61].

1.2 International Space Station

In considering the future of the International Space Station (ISS), the Committee asked two basic questions: What is the outlook between now and 2015? Should ISS be extended beyond 2015?

The Committee is concerned that the ISS, and particularly its utilization, may be vulnerable after Shuttle retirement. ISS was designed, assembled and operated with the capabilities of the Space Shuttle in mind. The present approach to its utilization is based on Shuttle-era experience. After Shuttle retirement, ISS will rely on a combination of new, and as yet unproven, international and commercial vehicles for cargo transport. Because the planned commercial resupply capability will be crucial to both ISS operations and utilization, it may be prudent to strengthen the incentives to the commercial providers to meet the schedule milestones.

Now that the ISS is nearly completed and is staffed by a full crew of six, its future success will depend on how well it is used. Up to now, the focus has been on assembling ISS, and this has come at the expense of using the Station. Utilization should have first priority in the years ahead.

The Committee finds that the return on investment of ISS to both the United States and the international partners would be significantly enhanced by an extension of ISS life to 2020. It seems unwise to de-orbit the Station after 25 years of assembly and only five years of operational life. Not to extend its operation would significantly impair U.S. ability to develop and lead future international spaceflight partnerships. Further, the ISS should be funded to enable it to achieve its full potential: as the nation's newest national laboratory, as an enhanced test bed for technologies and operational techniques that support exploration, and as a framework that can support expanded international collaboration.

The strong and tested working relationship among international partners is perhaps the most important outcome of the ISS program. The partnership expresses a "first among equals" U.S. leadership style adapted to today's multi-polar world. That leadership could extend to exploration, as the ISS partners

---

61   "Prior to operating the Shuttle beyond 2010, develop and conduct a vehicle recertification at the material, component, subsystem, and system levels. Recertification requirements should be included in the Service Life Extension Program." [Columbia Accident Investigation Board, R9.2-1]

could engage at an early stage if aspects of exploration beyond low-Earth orbit were included in the goals of the partnership agreement.

1.3 The Constellation Program

The Constellation Program includes: the Ares I launch vehicle, capable of launching astronauts to low-Earth orbit; the Ares V heavy-lift launch vehicle, to send astronauts and equipment to the Moon; the Orion capsule, intended to carry astronauts to low-Earth orbit and beyond; and the Altair lunar lander and lunar surface systems astronauts will need to explore the lunar surface. As the Committee assessed the current status and possible future of the Constellation Program, it reviewed the technical, budgetary and schedule challenges that the program faces today.

Given the funding originally expected, the Constellation Program was a reasonable architecture for human exploration. However, even when it was announced, its budget depended on funds becoming available from the retirement of the Space Shuttle in 2010 and the decommissioning of ISS in early 2016. Since then, as a result of technical and budgetary issues, the development schedules of Ares I and Orion have slipped, and work on Ares V and Altair has been delayed.

Most major vehicle-development programs face technical challenges as a normal part of the process, and Constellation is no exception. While significant, these are engineering problems, and the Committee expects that they can be solved. But these solutions may add to the program's cost and/or delay its schedule.

The original 2005 schedule showed Ares I and Orion available to support ISS in 2012, only two years after scheduled Shuttle retirement. The current schedule now shows that date as 2015. An independent assessment of the technical, budgetary and schedule risk to the Constellation Program performed for the Committee indicates that an additional delay of at least two years is likely.[62] This means that Ares I and Orion will not reach ISS before the Station's currently planned termination, and the length of the gap in U.S. ability to launch astronauts into space will be no less than seven years.

The Committee also examined the design and development of Orion. Many concepts are possible for crew-exploration vehicles, and NASA clearly needs a new spacecraft for travel beyond low-Earth orbit. The Committee found no compelling evidence that the current design will not be acceptable for its wide variety of tasks in the exploration program. However, the Committee

---

62   The independent assessment was conducted for the Committee by the Aerospace Corporation.

is concerned about Orion's recurring costs. The capsule is considerably larger and more massive than previous capsules (e.g., the Apollo capsule), and there is some indication that a smaller and lighter four-person Orion could reduce operational costs. However, a redesign of this magnitude would likely result in over a year of additional development time and a significant increase in cost, so such a redesign should be considered carefully before being implemented.

2.0 CABABILITY FOR LAUNCH TO LOW-EARTH ORBIT AND EXPLORATION BEYOND

2.1 Heavy-Lift Launch to Low-Earth Orbit and Beyond:

No one knows the mass or dimensions of the largest piece that will be required for future exploration missions, but it will likely be significantly larger than 25 metric tons (mt) in launch mass to low-Earth orbit, the capability of current launchers. As the size of the launcher increases, fewer launches and less operational complexity to assemble and/or refuel them results, and the net availability of launch capability increases. Combined with considerations of launch availability and on-orbit operations, the Committee finds that exploration will benefit from the availability of a heavy-lift vehicle. In addition, heavy lift would enable the launching of large scientific observatories and more capable deep-space missions. It may also provide benefit in national security applications. The question is: On what system should the next heavy-lift launch vehicle be based?

Family			Launch Mass to LEO
NASA Heritage	Ares Family	Ares V + Ares I	160 mt + 25 mt
		Ares V Lite	140 mt
	Shuttle Derived Family		100 - 110 mt
EELV Heritage Family			75 mt

Table 2-1. Characteristics of heavy-lift launch vehicles, indicating the EELV and NASA heritage families.

Potential approaches to developing heavy-lift vehicles (Table 2-1) are based on NASA heritage (Shuttle and Apollo) and EELV (evolved expendable launch vehicle) heritage. Each has its distinct advantages and disadvantages.

In the Ares-V-plus-Ares-I system planned by the Constellation program, the Ares I launches the Orion and docks in low-Earth orbit with the Altair lander launched on the Ares V. It has the advantage of projected very high ascent crew safety, but it delays the development of the Ares V heavy lift vehicle until after the independently operated Ares I is developed.

In a different, related architecture, the Orion and Altair are launched on two separate "Lite" versions of the Ares V, providing for more robust mass margins. Building a single NASA vehicle could reduce carrying and operations costs, and accelerate heavy-lift development. Of these two Ares system alternatives, the Committee finds the Ares V Lite in the dual mode the preferred reference option.

The more directly Shuttle-derived family consists of in-line and side-mount vehicles substantially derived from the Shuttle, providing more continuity in workforce. The development cost of the more Shuttle-derived system would be lower, but it would be less capable than the Ares V family and have higher recurring costs. The lower launch capability could eventually be offset by developing on-orbit refueling.

The EELV-heritage systems have the least lift capability, so that to provide equal performance, almost twice as many launches would be required, when compared to the Ares family. If on-orbit refueling were developed and used, the number of launches could be reduced, but operational complexity would be added. However, the EELV approach would also represent a new way of doing business for NASA, which would have the benefit of potentially lowering development and operational costs. This would come at the cost of ending a substantial portion of the internal NASA capability to develop and operate launchers. It would also require that NASA and the Department of Defense jointly develop the new system.

All of the options would benefit from the development of in-space refueling, and the smaller rockets would benefit most of all. The potential government-guaranteed market for fuel in low-Earth orbit would create a stimulus to the commercial launch industry. In the design of the new launcher, in-space stages and in-space refueling, the Committee cautions against the tradition of designing for ultimate performance, at the cost of reliability, operational efficiency and life-cycle cost.

2.2 Crew Access to Low-Earth Orbit

How should U.S. astronauts be transported to low-Earth orbit? There are two basic approaches: a government-operated system and a commercial crew-delivery service. The current Constellation Program plan is to use the government-operated Ares I launch vehicle and the Orion crew capsule.

However, the Committee found that, because of technical and budget issues, the Ares I schedule no longer supports the ISS.

Ares I was designed to a high standard in order to provide astronauts with access to low-Earth orbit at lower risk and a considerably higher level of reliability than is available today. To achieve this, it uses a high-reliability rocket and a crew capsule with a launch-escape system. But other potential combinations of high-reliability rockets and capsules with escape systems could also provide that reliability. The Committee was unconvinced that enough is known about any of the potential high-reliability launcher-plus-capsule systems to distinguish their levels of safety in a meaningful way.

The United States needs a way to launch astronauts to low-Earth orbit, but it does not necessarily have to be provided by the government. As we move from the complex, reusable Shuttle back to a simpler, smaller capsule, it is an appropriate time to consider turning this transport service over to the commercial sector. This approach is not without technical and programmatic risks, but it creates the possibility of lower operating costs for the system and potentially accelerates the availability of U.S. access to low-Earth orbit by about a year, to 2016. The Committee suggests establishing a new competition for this service, in which both large and small companies could participate.

2.3 Lowering the cost of space exploration

The cost of exploration is dominated by the costs of launch to low-Earth orbit and of the in-space systems. It seems improbable that significant reductions in launch costs will be realized in the short term until launch rates increase substantially—perhaps through expanded commercial activity in space. How can the nation stimulate such activity? In the 1920s, the federal government awarded a series of guaranteed contracts for carrying airmail, stimulating the growth of the airline industry. The Committee concludes that an architecture for exploration employing a similar policy of guaranteed contracts has the potential to stimulate a vigorous and competitive commercial space industry. Such commercial ventures could include supply of cargo to the ISS (already underway), transport of crew to orbit and transport of fuel to orbit. Establishing these commercial opportunities could increase launch volume and potentially lower costs to NASA and all other launch-services customers.

This would have the additional benefit of focusing NASA on a more challenging role, permitting it to concentrate its efforts where its inherent capability resides: for example, developing cutting-edge technologies and concepts, and defining programs and overseeing the development and operation of exploration systems, particularly those beyond low-Earth orbit.

The Committee strongly believes it is time for NASA to reassume its crucial role of developing new technologies for space. Today, the alternatives available for exploration systems are severely limited because of the lack of a strategic investment in technology development in past decades. NASA now has an opportunity to develop a technology roadmap that is aligned with an exploration mission that will last for decades. If appropriately funded, a technology development program would re-engage the minds at American universities, in industry and within NASA. The investments should be designed to increase the capabilities and reduce the costs of future exploration. This will benefit human and robotic exploration, the commercial space community, and other U.S. government users.

3.0 FUTURE DESTINATIONS FOR EXPLORATION

What is the strategy for exploration beyond low-Earth orbit? Humans could embark on the following paths to explore the inner solar system:

Mars first, with a Mars landing, perhaps after a brief test of equipment and procedures on the Moon.

Moon first, with lunar surface exploration focused on developing the capability to explore Mars.

Flexible path to inner solar system locations, such as lunar orbit, Lagrange points, near-Earth objects and the moons of Mars, followed by exploration of the lunar surface and/or Martian surface.

A human landing followed by an extended human presence on Mars stands prominently above all other opportunities for exploration. Mars is unquestionably the most scientifically interesting destination in the inner solar system, with a history much like Earth's. It possesses resources, which can be used for life support and propellants. If humans are ever to live for long periods on another planetary surface, it is likely to be on Mars. But Mars is not an easy place to visit with existing technology and without a substantial investment of resources. The Committee finds that Mars is the ultimate destination for human exploration; but it is not the best first destination.

What about the Moon first, then Mars? By first exploring the Moon, we could develop the operational skills and technology for landing on, launching from and working on a planetary surface. In the process, we could acquire an understanding of human adaptation to another world that would one day allow us to go to Mars.

There are two main strategies for exploring the Moon. Both begin with a few short sorties to various sites to scout the region and validate the lunar landing and ascent systems. In one strategy, the next step would be to build a base. Over many missions, a small colony of habitats would be assembled, and explorers would begin to live there for many months, conducting scientific studies and prospecting for resources that could be used as fuel. In the other strategy, sorties would continue to different sites, spending weeks and then months at each one. More equipment would have to be brought on each trip, but more diverse sites would be explored and in greater detail.

There is a third possible path for human exploration beyond low-Earth orbit, which the Committee calls the Flexible Path. On this path, humans would visit sites never visited before and extend our knowledge of how to operate in space—while traveling greater and greater distances from Earth. Successive missions would visit: lunar orbit; the Lagrange points (special points in space that are important sites for scientific observations and the future space transportation infrastructure); near-Earth objects (asteroids that cross the Earth's path); and orbit around Mars. Most interestingly, humans could rendezvous with a moon of Mars, then coordinate with or control robots on the Martian surface.

The Flexible Path represents a different type of exploration strategy. We would learn how to live and work in space, to visit small bodies, and to work with robotic probes on the planetary surface. It would provide the public and other stakeholders with a series of interesting "firsts" to keep them engaged and supportive. Most important, because the path is flexible, it would allow many different options as exploration progresses, including a return to the Moon's surface, or a continuation to the surface of Mars. The Committee finds that both Moon First and Flexible Path are viable exploration strategies. It also finds that they are not necessarily mutually exclusive; before traveling to Mars, we might be well served to both extend our presence in free space and gain experience working on the lunar surface.

4.0 INTEGRATED PROGRAM OPTIONS

The Committee has identified five principal alternatives for the human spaceflight program. They include one baseline case, which the Committee believes to be an executable version of the current program of record, funded to achieve its stated exploration goals, as well as four alternatives. These options are summarized in Table 4-1.

	Budget	Shuttle Life	ISS Life	Heavy Launch	Crew to LEO
Constrained Options					
Option 1: Program of Record (constrained)	FY10 Budget	2011	2015	Ares V	Ares I + Orion
Option 2: ISS + Lunar (constrained)	FY10 Budget	2011	2020	Ares V Lite	Commercial
Moon First Options					
Option 3: Baseline - Program of Record	Less Constrained	2011	2015	Ares V	Ares I + Orion
Option 4A: Moon First - Ares Lite	Less Constrained	2011	2020	Ares V Lite	Commercial
Option 4B Moon First - Extended Shuttle	Less Constrained	2015	2020	Direct Shuttle Derived + refueling	Commercial
Flexible Path Options					
Option 5A: Flexible Path - Ares Lite	Less Constrained	2011	2020	Ares V Lite	Commercial
Option 5B: Flexible Path - EELV Heritage	Less Constrained	2011	2020	75mt EELV + refueling	Commercial
Option 5C: Flexible Path - Shuttle Derived	Less Constrained	2011	2020	Direct Shuttle Derived + refueling	Commercial

Note: Program-of-Record derived options (Options 1 and 3) do not contain technology program; all others do.

Table 4-1. A summary of the integrated program options.

The committee was asked to provide two options that fit within the FY 2010 budget profile. This funding is essentially flat or decreasing through 2014, then increases at 1.4 percent per year

thereafter, which is less than the 2.4 percent per year used to estimate cost inflation. The first two options are constrained to that budget.

Option 1. Program of Record as assessed by the Committee, constrained to the FY 2010 budget. This option is the Program of Record, with only two changes the Committee deems necessary: providing funds for the Shuttle into FY 2011 and including sufficient funds to de-orbit the ISS in 2016. When constrained to this budget profile, Ares I and Orion are not available until after the ISS has been de-orbited. The heavy-lift vehicle, Ares V, is not available until the late 2020s, and worse, there are insufficient funds to develop the lunar lander and lunar surface systems until well into the 2030s, if ever.

Option 2. ISS and Lunar Exploration, constrained to FY 2010 budget. This option extends the ISS to 2020, and it begins a program of lunar exploration using Ares V (Lite). The option assumes Shuttle fly-out in FY 2011, and it includes a technology development program, a program to develop commercial crew services to low-Earth orbit, and funds for enhanced utilization of ISS. This option does not deliver heavy-lift capability until the late 2020s and does not have funds to develop the systems needed to land on or explore the Moon.

The remaining three alternatives are fit to a different budget profile—one that the Committee judged more appropriate for an exploration program designed to carry humans beyond low-Earth orbit. This budget increases to $3 billion above the FY 2010 guidance by FY 2014, then grows with inflation at a more reasonable 2.4 percent per year.

Option 3. Baseline Case —Implementable Program of Record. This is an executable version of the program of record. It consists of the content and sequence of that program – de-orbiting the ISS in 2016, developing Orion, Ares I and Ares V, and beginning exploration of the Moon. The Committee made only two additions it felt essential: budgeting for the fly-out of the Shuttle in 2011 and including additional funds for ISS de-orbit. The Committee's assessment is that, under this funding profile, the option delivers Ares1/Orion in FY 2017, with human lunar return in the mid- 2020s.

Option 4. Moon First. This option preserves the Moon as the first destination for human exploration beyond low-Earth orbit. It also extends the ISS to 2020, funds technology advancement, and uses commercial vehicles to carry crew to low-Earth orbit. There are two significantly different variants to this option.

Variant 4A is the Ares Lite variant. This retires the Shuttle in FY 2011 and develops the Ares V (Lite) heavy-lift launcher for lunar exploration. *Variant 4B* is the Shuttle extension variant. This variant includes the only foreseeable way to eliminate the gap in U.S. human-launch capability: it extends the Shuttle to 2015 at a minimum safe-flight rate. It also takes advantage of synergy with the Shuttle by developing a heavy-lift vehicle that is more directly Shuttle-derived. Both variants of Option 4 permit human lunar return by the mid-2020s.

Option 5. Flexible Path. This option follows the Flexible Path as an exploration strategy. It operates the Shuttle into FY 2011, extends the ISS until 2020, funds technology development and develops commercial crew services to low-Earth orbit. There are three variants within this option; they differ only in the heavy-lift vehicle.

Variant 5A is the Ares Lite variant. It develops the Ares Lite, the most capable of the heavylift vehicles in this option. *Variant 5B* employs an EELV-heritage commercial heavy-lift launcher and assumes a different (and significantly reduced) role for NASA. It has an advantage of potentially lower operational costs, but requires significant restructuring of NASA. *Variant 5C* uses a directly Shuttle-derived, heavy-lift vehicle, taking maximum advantage of existing infrastructure, facilities and production capabilities.

All variants of Option 5 begin exploration along the flexible path in the early 2020s, with lunar fly-bys, visits to Lagrange points and near-Earth objects and Mars fly-bys occurring at a rate of about one major event per year, and possible rendezvous with Mars's moons or human lunar return by the mid to late 2020s.

The Committee has found two executable options that comply with the FY 2010 budget. However, neither allows for a viable exploration program. In fact, the Committee finds that no plan compatible with the FY 2010 budget profile permits human exploration to continue in any meaningful way.

The Committee further finds that it is possible to conduct a viable exploration program with a budget rising to about $3 billion annually above the FY 2010 budget profile. At this budget level, both the Moon First strategy and the Flexible Path strategies begin human exploration on a reasonable, though hardly aggressive, timetable. The Committee believes an exploration program that will be a source of pride for the nation requires resources at such a level.

5.0 ORGANIZATIONAL AND PROGRAMMATIC ISSUES

How might NASA organize to explore? The NASA Administrator needs to be given the authority to manage NASA's resources, including its workforce and facilities. Even the bestmanaged human spaceflight programs will encounter developmental problems. Such activities must be adequately funded, including reserves to account for the unforeseen and unforeseeable. Good management is especially difficult when funds cannot be moved from one human spaceflight budget line to another—and where new funds can ordinarily be obtained only after a two-year delay (if at all). NASA should be given the maximum flexibility possible under the law to establish and manage its systems.

Finally, significant space achievements require continuity of support over many years. One way to ensure that no successes are achieved is to continually pull up the flowers to see if the roots are healthy. (This Committee might be accused of being part of this pattern!) NASA and its human spaceflight program are in need of stability in both resources and direction.

6.0 SUMMARY OF KEY FINDINGS

The Committee summarizes its key findings below. Additional findings are included in the body of the report.

The right mission and the right size: NASA's budget should match its mission and goals. Further, NASA should be given the ability to shape its organization and infrastructure accordingly, while maintaining facilities deemed to be of national importance.

International partnerships: The U.S. can lead a bold new international effort in the human exploration of space. If international partners are actively engaged, including on the "critical path" to success, there could be substantial benefits to foreign relations, and more resources overall could become available.

Short-term Space Shuttle planning: The current Shuttle manifest should be flown in a safe and prudent manner. The current manifest will likely extend to the second quarter of FY 2011. It is important to budget for this likelihood.

The human-spaceflight gap: Under current conditions, the gap in U.S. ability to launch astronauts into space will stretch to at least seven years. The Committee did not identify any credible approach employing new capabilities that could shorten the gap to less than six years. The only way to significantly close the gap is to extend the life of the Shuttle Program.

Extending the International Space Station: The return on investment to both the United States and our international partners would be significantly enhanced by an extension of ISS life. Not to extend its operation would significantly impair U.S. ability to develop and lead future international spaceflight partnerships.

Heavy-lift: A heavy-lift launch capability to low-Earth orbit, combined with the ability to inject heavy payloads away from the Earth, is beneficial to exploration, and it also will be useful to the national security space and scientific communities. The Committee reviewed: the Ares family of launchers; more directly Shuttle-derived vehicles; and launchers derived from the EELV family. Each approach has advantages and disadvantages, trading capability, lifecycle costs, operational complexity and the "way of doing business" within the program and NASA.

Commercial crew launch to low-Earth orbit: Commercial services to deliver crew to low-Earth orbit are within reach. While this presents some risk, it could provide an earlier capability at lower initial and lifecycle costs than government could achieve. A new competition with adequate incentives should be open to all U.S. aerospace companies. This would allow NASA to focus on more challenging roles, including human exploration beyond low-Earth orbit, based on the continued development of the current or modified Orion spacecraft.

Technology development for exploration and commercial space: Investment in a well-designed and adequately funded space technology program is critical to enable progress in exploration. Exploration strategies can proceed more readily and economically if the requisite technology has been developed in advance. This investment will also benefit robotic exploration, the U.S. commercial space industry and other U.S. government users.

Pathways to Mars: Mars is the ultimate destination for human exploration; but it is not the best first destination. Both visiting the Moon First and following the Flexible Path are viable exploration strategies. The two are not necessarily mutually exclusive; before traveling to Mars, we might be well served to both extend our presence in free space and gain experience working on the lunar surface.

Options for the Human Spaceflight Program: The Committee developed five alternatives for the Human Spaceflight Program. It found:

Human exploration beyond low-Earth orbit is not viable under the FY 2010 budget guideline.

Meaningful human exploration is possible under a less constrained budget, ramping to approximately $3 billion per year above the FY 2010 guidance in total resources.

Funding at the increased level would allow either an exploration program to explore Moon First or one that follows a Flexible Path of exploration. Either could produce results in a reasonable timeframe.

Chapter Eight

Deadly Vanguards: A study of al-Qa'ida's Violence against Muslims

December 2009
By
Scott Helfstein, Ph.D.
Nassir Abdullah
Muhammad al-Obaidi

The views expressed in this report are the authors' and do not reflect those of the U.S. Military Academy, the Department of Defense, or the U.S. Government. The first 62 notes and the narrative are excluded here

> *"We haven't killed the innocents; not in Baghdad, nor in Morocco, nor in Algeria, nor anywhere else. And if there is any innocent who was killed in the Mujahideen's operations, then it was either an unintentional error, or out of necessity as in cases of al-Tatarrus."*
>
> *Ayman al-Zawahiri*
> *The Power of Truth, 2007*

In a 2007 online forum, al-Qa'ida's second in command Ayman al-Zawahiri, confronted questions about the organization's use of violence and especially violence against Muslims. Zawahiri and other leaders have defended al-Qa'ida's use of violence, arguing that their operations do not kill Muslims, and on the rare occasions they do, such individuals are apostates or martyrs. Since the inception of al-Qa'ida, the organization has claimed to represent Muslim interests around the world declaring itself the vanguard of true Islam, and the defender of Muslim people. Unfortunately for al-Qa'ida, their actions speak louder than their words. The fact is that the vast majority of al-Qa'ida's victims are Muslims: the analysis here shows that only 15% of the fatalities resulting from al-Qa'ida attacks between 2004 and 2008 were Westerners.[63]

The results show that non-Westerners are much more likely to be killed in an al-Qa'ida attack. From 2004 to 2008, only 15% percent of the 3,010 victims were Western. During the most recent period studied the numbers skew even further. From 2006 to 2008, only 2% (12 of 661 victims) are from the West, and the remaining 98% are inhabitants of countries with Muslim majorities. During this period, a person of non-Western origin was 54 times more likely to die in an al-Qa'ida attack than an individual from the West. The overwhelming majority of al-Qa'ida victims are Muslims living in Muslim countries, and many are citizens of Iraq, which suffered more al-Qa'ida attacks than any other country courtesy of the al-Qa'ida in Iraq (AQI) affiliate.

It is interesting to note that the percentage of non-Western victims increased in the more recent period at the same time that extremist scholars, pundits, and supporters are questioning the indiscriminate use of violence and the targeting of Muslims. Al-Qa'ida leaders stress that these individuals are not formal members of the organization, but recognizes their legitimacy as scholars and intellectual contributions to the movement nonetheless.[64] One of the most referenced actors in the movement, Abu Muhammad al-Maqdisi, abandoned his support of takfir (the practice of excommunication that is often used to justify murder), and condemned al-Qa'ida for indiscriminate killing.[65] Even pundits that continue to support al-Qa'ida's vision of jihad and the use of takfir still warn against the adverse effects of targeting Muslims. For example, Nadj al-Rawi, a well-regarded jihadist pundit, warns that excessive declaration of takfir may generate "antagonism of a Muslim toward his religion."[66] Sheikh Hamed bin Abdullah al-Ali, former Secretary General of the Salafi Movement of Kuwait, counseled jihadis to recognize the sanctity of Muslim blood.[67] Even one of al-Qa'ida's important senior leaders, Abu Yahya al-Libi, alluded to

---

63 This time period is a product of the open source database on terrorist incidents, running from 2004 to the current, and is discussed in the section below. The report also examines some additional major al-Qa'ida attacks in prior periods.

64 Ayman al-Zawahiri, "The Facts of Jihad and the Lies of Hypocrisy," interview, 3 August 2009.

65 Abu Muhammad al-Maqdisi's, "Support and Advice, Pains and Hopes," July 2004, a message to Abu Musab al-Zarqawi.

66 Atta Najd al-Rawi, "An Answer to a Question From the Holy Land," 1 March 2008. Translation from the SITE Institute.

67 Hamed al-Ali, "The Covenant of the Supreme Council of Jihad Groups (Mithaq al-Majles al-A'la li-Fasael al-Jihad)," January 2007.

operational mistakes that might alienate the broader population, and blamed the Ullema (Muslim clerics) for poor guidance and support.[68]

Despite numerous warnings and ongoing public debates about the indiscriminate use of violence, al-Qa'ida remains committed to its current tactics as displayed by the steady stream of Muslim fatalities from 2006 to 2008. Al-Qa'ida was marginally successful at attacking Westerners in 2004 and 2005, largely resulting from the attacks in Madrid and London. However, attacks dropped off considerably in 2006, and there were no Western fatalities recorded from al-Qa'ida attacks in that year. In 2007 and 2008 attacks leveled off to 30 and 29, respectively, but there are almost no Western fatalities (12 of 571 victims). Irrespective of statements made by Zawahiri and others, the figures, drawn from exclusively Arabic news sources, show that the Muslims they claim to protect are much more likely to be the targets of al-Qa'ida violence than the Western powers they claim to fight.

Methodology: Arabic Primary Source Material

One of the most important aspects of this work is the research method employed to generate the data tables used in the analysis and found in the appendix. As noted above, many analytical pieces on terrorist incidents, from both academia and government, rely exclusively on open source English language material. This project differs by drawing on Arabic language primary source material. The use of such source material will hopefully add fidelity to analytical conclusions about al-Qa'ida's targeting and victims.

Since the 11 September attacks, various government and academic institutions have invested in the development of comprehensive data sources on terrorist incidents worldwide.[69] A comprehensive study or review of the different data sources is beyond the scope of this paper, but it is important to understand some of the difficulties that arise in such an endeavor.[70] First, there is debate about what exactly constitutes a terrorist incident, and different data sources have different rules for inclusion. Some datasets rely on real-time event coding, and others incorporate data in a historical or retrospective process.[71]

---

68 Abu Yahya al-Libi, "Jihadist Forum Member Posts Al-Libi Interview with Al-Sahab, 2002" 28 July 2009.

69 This work built upon already existent datasets such as ITERATE, which tracks transnational attacks, and the RAND incident set which was not publicly available.

70 Note that this is not an exhaustive list of issues or difficulties. Those interested should examine the coding methodologies associated with the existing datasets.

71 Note two representative datasets: the Worldwide Incident Tracking System

Second, different primary source material often has different accounts of the same event. Fatalities, locations, or perpetrators may vary among sources, though that variance is usually small amongst credible sources. Nevertheless, even slight variance complicates coding since researchers have to acquire a number of sources to gain confidence in their records. Third, attack attribution remains difficult. Attribution is easiest when perpetrators claim responsibility (though in some cases multiple groups may lay claim to a successful attack), but information is often sparse and contradictory on attacks conducted anonymously. Finally, the different coding rules employed by different institutions make it difficult to merge the different data sources. One group might consider an incident a terrorist attack, where another might exclude the attack because of different coding rules or heuristics. This complicates analysis across datasets, and helps justify the use of such sources as standalone resources rather than trying to integrate between them.

The data in the tables attached to this report is from Arabic primary source news material, but the research team generated the initial list of attacks using the Worldwide Incident Tracking System (WITS).[72] The WITS database is an open source dataset of terrorism incidents maintained by the National Counterterrorism Center. The team in charge of maintaining WITS details the methodology it uses to generate the dataset, attempting to ensure transparency in its coding process. The WITS dataset was only used to generate the initial list of al-Qa'ida attacks (date and place), and was not used to generate the fatality data discussed below. The WITS dataset went online in 2004 and covers the period from 2004 to 2009 (updates are posted quarterly). To ensure that al-Qa'ida's targeting from 2004 to 2008 remained reasonably consistent over the operational life of the group, the analysis also examines a small set of high profile attacks from the late 1990s and early 2000s. This additional data is discussed in greater detail below.

There were two criteria used to generate the list of attacks: 1) the attack had to be carried out by al-Qa'ida or a group publicly associated with al-Qa'ida, and 2) the perpetrators needed to claim responsibility for the attack.[73] The rationale for this approach is reasonably straightforward. First, the report details the activity of al-Qa'ida and its associates rather than all terrorist and insurgent groups more broadly. Second, attribution is difficult, making it

---

uses real-time event coding (every month additional events are added and incidents are updated as new information comes available), and the Global Terrorism Database uses a retrospective process (acquiring historical information in larger increments and scrutinizing its accuracy).

72   The WITS dataset can be accessed at http://wits.nctc.gov/.

73   The search excluded all attacks where no one claimed responsibility then filtered for al-Qa'ida participation.

important to minimize the number of attacks included where the perpetrators are not self-identifying.[74] Self-identification is an important element in this report. In many instances, one might imagine that perpetrators were most likely to claim responsibility for attacks they are proud of and avoid such claims when they are displeased by the outcome. Al-Qa'ida's ability to exploit other actors or manipulate situations behind the scenes, as the group has done in Afghanistan and Pakistan, make it more difficult to identify all of the attacks that tie back to that organization, but al-Qa'ida should still be incentivized to avoid claiming responsibility when outcomes are poor. By limiting this dataset to attacks with claims of responsibility, the report should capture the attacks that al-Qa'ida and its associates are most proud of, presumably meaning attacks against Western targets, and under report the total number of attacks in places such as Pakistan. This data inclusion and search rule helps to ensure that violence against non-Westerners is most likely underreported in the data and resulting analytics.

After generating the list of attack dates, the research team exploited the large cache of Arabic news sources available online. Rather than use casualty data from the WITS (or any other) system, this study wanted to differentiate itself from many of the other databases by using Arabic news sources that are widely available. Each attack observation was used to search for articles or incident records from the Arabic news sources, with hope of culling information about the attack victims. Each time the Arabic press reported an event the researcher coded the number of fatalities, the number of Western versus non-Western fatalities, and the news source used in the study.[75] In many instances, multiple news sources were used to ensure accuracy.

The initial list of al-Qa'ida attacks included 329 incidents. Within this list, researchers were unable to find Arabic news citations for 16 (4.8%) of the incidents. Of these unsubstantiated records, other datasets reported that there were no fatalities in ten of the incidents, and one fatality in each of three incidents. This suggests that the difficulty associated with finding Arabic news sources may lend more to the small scale of these attacks relative to

---

74 The WITS system does not directly code the perpetrator as a data field, but it is included in the event description. Coding a single perpetrator is difficult since groups may collaborate.

75 The coding scheme used for this project focused on nationality, relying on designation of victims as "Western" and "non-Western." This scheme was used because media sources (irrespective of language) usually include victims' nationalities as identifying religious affiliation is difficult. It is interesting to note that if major media outlets cannot distinguish victims' religions, it is difficult to believe that others (such published jihadi materials) could obtain an accurate assessment.

the vast numbers of attacks that occur. The most deadly attack among those apparently not reported by the Arabic media resulted in 15 fatalities. All of these attacks are still listed in the data table found in the appendix, but they are not included in the analytics below. The low number of casualties in the set of unreported incidents means that inclusion would not impact the analytic results in any meaningful way. The research team could have relied on other existing data sources to incorporate these attacks, but it was important that the team be able to generate the data off the primary Arabic source material. If Arabic open source reporting did not capture the event, it is treated as though it did not happen for the analytics below.

After using this process for the incidents from 2004 to 2008, researchers examined an additional set of al-Qa'ida attacks to ensure that the results from this more recent period (2004-2008) were consistent with prior behavior (1995-2003). There were 23 attacks, some high profile, perpetrated from 1995 to 2003. The outcome of these attacks was then coded using the same methodology described above. This list of attacks, fatalities, and the open source Arabic media sources used to code fatalities is included in the appendix.

Analytics: The Real Victims

From 2004 to 2008, there were 3,010 fatalities in 313 attacks. On average, there were 9.6 people killed per attack during this period, and this remains reasonably consistent from 2004 to 2007. The fatalities per attack decline in 2008, averaging 7.2 people killed per incident. Over the entire five year period, Arabic news sources revealed that only 12% (371) of al-Qa'ida's victims were Westerners. Excluding the Madrid bombings on 11 March 2004 and the London bombings on 7 July 2005, the Arabic media sources used here show that only 4.4% of al-Qa'ida's victims were Western.[76] Including or excluding these two attacks, it is clear that al-Qa'ida's violence disproportionately harms the Muslim community. This section takes a closer look at the data and identifies some trends. Total casualties from al-Qa'ida attacks have fluctuated in the period under study. One reason for the observed fluctuation in fatalities is the high levels of violence in Iraq around 2005. Figure 1 shows the total casualties annually from 2004 to 2008 characterized as Western and non-Western, with the total number of incidents for each year listed along the bottom axis in the parentheses. The analysis shows that the variation in casualties fluctuated with the variation in incidents, which is not surprising.

---

76 The sources used reflected 197 Westerners killed in the Madrid attack and 52 killed in the London attack.

The number of attacks leveled off in 2007 and 2008, with 30 and 29 attacks, respectively. The chart also shows that the number of Western victims is disproportionately low relative to the total fatalities over the entire period. Figure 2 shows the annual casualties by percentage, and supports the notion that Westerners are unlikely to fall victim to al-Qa'ida attacks.

Figure 1: Casualties, Annual

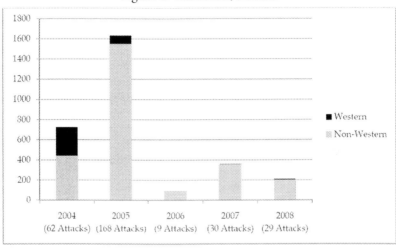

Figure 2: Casualty Percentage, Annual

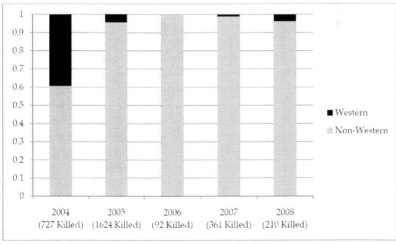

Monthly causalities for the period 2004 to 2008 are found in Figure 3. They show two clear trends: 1) there is high variance in the number of people killed each month, and 2) the number of Western casualties is far below the non-Western casualties in every month except March 2004 (the first month recorded in the study). The variation in casualties from month to month reflects the opportunistic nature of al-Qa'ida and terrorism. Terror groups attack when they have the will and capability, and the variation suggests that their capability to attack waxes and wanes with time. Given al-Qa'ida's need to strike in order to maintain relevance, it is not surprising that it is not discerning in its targeting. This argument gains further support when one looks at the distribution of casualties by country, shown in Figure 4. Since al-Qa'ida has limited capability to strike against its Western enemies, the group maintains its relevance by attacking countries with Muslim majorities.

Figure 3: Casualties, Monthly

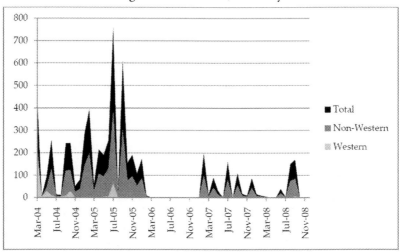

Figure 4: Casualties, By Country (Excluding Iraq)

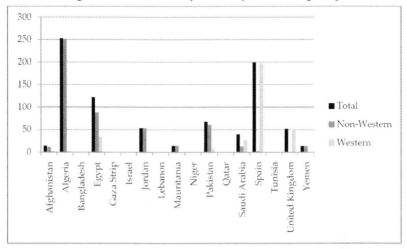

Note: Iraq is excluded from this figure because the number of casualties is disproportionately high when compared to the other countries targeted in al-Qa'ida attacks.

One could argue that non-Western casualties in Iraq and Afghanistan are unfortunate martyrs or collateral damage given the ongoing wars initiated by the United States. Excluding the Afghan and Iraqi theaters from the analysis, the data shows that 39 percent of al-Qa'ida's victims are Westerners, a significant increase over the 4% shown above. Yet if one were to remove the Madrid and London attacks, outside of Iraq and Afghanistan Westerners account for only 13% of al-Qa'ida's victims. Most recently, al-Qa'ida's targeting has grown increasingly indiscriminate. Outside of the war zones of Afghanistan and Iraq, 99% of al-Qa'ida's victims were non-Western in 2007, and 96% were non-Western in 2008. From 2006 to 2008, only 9 of 352 victims were Westerners (3%), meaning that non-Westerners were 38 times more likely to die in an al-Qa'ida attack outside of Iraq and Afghanistan during those years. Figure 5 shows the annual breakdown in casualties excluding Afghanistan and Iraq.

Figure 5: Casualties, Excluding Afghanistan and Iraq, Annual

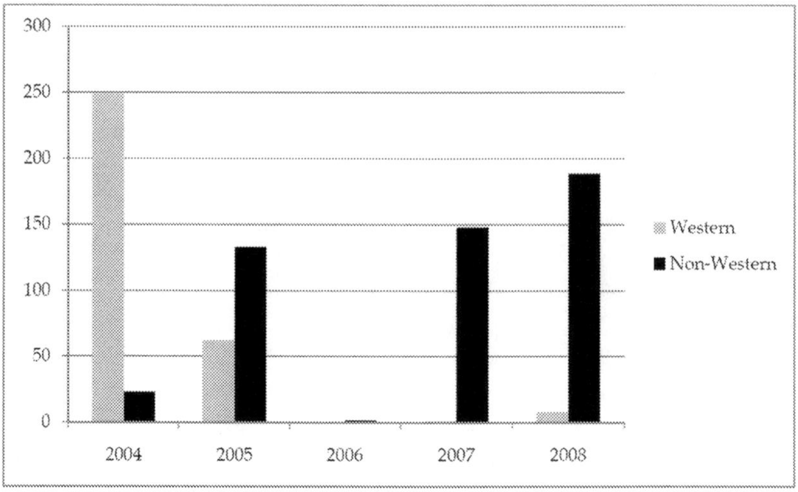

Across all the incidents recorded, total fatalities from al-Qa'ida attacks during this period reflect a power law distribution as displayed in Figure 6. Power law applies to situations where few events account for the most casualties, and many events create very few casualties. There are many attacks with no or very few causalities, and a few attacks that are exceptionally deadly. This pattern is common and applies to wartime causalities as well as other analyses of terror attack casualties, and al-Qa'ida attacks are no exception. This behavior suggests that al-Qa'ida is no different from any rogue, criminal, or rebel terrorist group.

Figure 6: Number of Attacks by Fatality

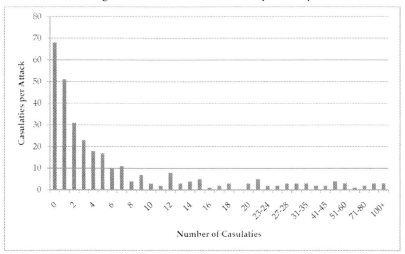

It is possible that the trends observed from 2004 to 2008 are an aberration, and evidence from prior periods reflects that al-Qa'ida is more selective in its targeting. To confirm that the results presented above are robust across the life of the organization, researchers used the same analytical method to generate casualties on a list of major al-Qa'ida attacks from 1995 to 2003. The results and sources are also found in the appendix. In that period, there were 23 al-Qa'ida attacks and 20 of 23 took place in countries with Muslim majorities, the remaining three took place on 9/11. In that period there 3,454 casualties, 3,021 of which were produced in the 9/11 attacks. Excluding that attack, Arabic sources report 433 casualties for the period and only 19% (82) of those were Westerners. This is displayed in Figure 7, which shows the total casualties during the period, and the casualties excluding the 9/11 attacks. Compared to the more recent period, al-Qa'ida was marginally better at targeting Westerners, but if one excludes the 9/11 attacks, the majority of the victims were still non-Western. Hence, the trends reflected from 1995 to 2003 do not differ significantly from those in 2004 to 2008, excluding 9/11, and the comparison shows that al-Qa'ida is growing more violent and less discriminate.

Figure 7: Casualties 1995-2003, Including and Excluding the 9/11 Attack

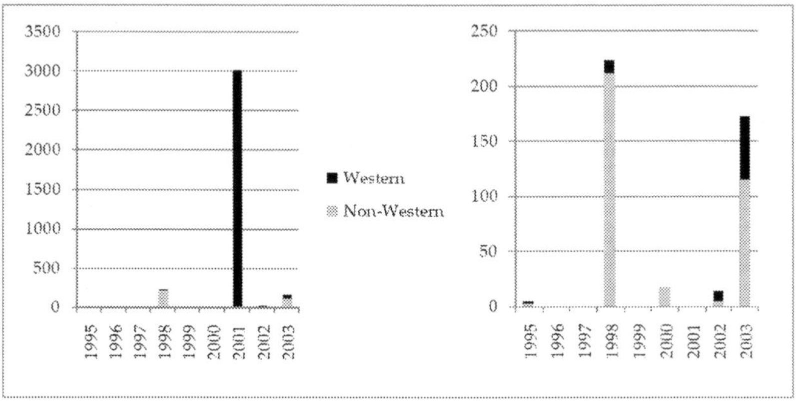

Conclusions

Irrespective of the ongoing public debates about takfir and violence against Muslims amongst al-Qa'ida associates, deeds speak louder than words. Al-Qa'ida represents itself as the vanguard of the Muslim community, committed to upholding Islamic values and defending Muslim people against Western forces, but its behavior represents a callous attitude toward the lives of those the group claims to protect. Al-Qa'ida absolves responsibility for the deaths of Muslims by claiming that they are either martyrs or apostates. The definition of apostate, however, varies considerably. Al-Qa'ida considers any Muslim that impedes their struggle by working with the West or an unfriendly regime as an apostate, and therefore a legitimate target. This includes Muslims serving in the armed forces, serving as police officers, and even those occupying civilian jobs. Al-Qa'ida makes convenient use of this designation to justify its indiscriminate use of violence.

To justify the killing of innocent Muslims, or martyrs, al-Qa'ida references a shari'a rule called al-tatarrus. Al-tatarrus refers to the use of human shields, the practice of avoiding hostility by hiding behind others. Muslims are not supposed to kill other Muslims, and historically, enemies used this prohibition against Muslim military forces by surrounding themselves with other Muslims. Muslims found the al-tatarrus rule was a strategic liability and looked for ways to circumvent the ban. The notion that it is okay to kill Muslims being used as human shields, is not widely invoked or discussed in other contemporary circles. Al-Qa'ida resurrected the term to justify the killing of innocents, arguing that these people were essentially human shields, and if innocent, they died martyrs. Among the only justifications for this obscure rule is Abu

Yahya al-Libi's book entitled "Al-Tatarrus in the Modern Jihad," and Ayman al-Zawhiri cited this source during his open forum referenced above.[77] Al-Qa'ida has acknowledged that assailants should be patient and wait for the right time to carry out attacks (in martyr videos and announcements), but this report shows there is scant evidence of prudence or effort to limit violence. Irrespective of al-Qa'ida's justifications, if history provides a glimpse into the future, the group and its associates will pose the greatest threat to fellow Muslims.

---

77 Jarret Brachman and Brian Fishman, The Power of Truth (West Point, NY: Combating Terrorism Center, 2007), p. 6.

CHAPTER NINE

WHY THE WAR CAME - LINCOLN AND THE LORDS OF THE LASH

By
Michael P. Riccards

This year marks the 150th anniversary of the start of the Civil War. We have here in New Jersey a group that is planning activities to celebrate that beginning of the conflict; they are men and women who will hail the eventual triumph of the North in that terrible conflict. But any historical memory brings revisionists, and in some areas of the South, the Sons and Daughters of the Confederacy are actually having balls and parties to hail their secessionist forbearers.

What really should not be permitted though is the attempt to distort history so that we say that the War had nothing to do with slavery, that is that the "Noble Cause," as they call it, was not fought to keep people enslaved from birth to death. To argue that the real issue was simply states' rights is a gross fabrication. The leaders of the Confederacy were clear in their own minds that slavery was the core issue. Sometime ago I had the opportunity to give a public lecture in Massachusetts on the controversy, for it is not new nor is it valid. The Southern leaders were clear they fought the war to preserve their "peculiar institution." They were more candid than their children's grandchildren are.

The Civil War is our Iliad and our Odyssey, our chronicle of war and return, of fratricidal conflict and of uneasy reconciliation. Since then historians have debated at length the causes of that war, and there is no real consensus as to why the North and the South finally split asunder. Scholars have cited so many reasons – simple and complex – that we have sometimes forgotten what the contemporaries of those times observed.

One of the most perceptive participants was, of course, Abraham Lincoln, and after four years of terrible destruction, he judged in his second inaugural address:

"Both parties depreciated war; but one of them would make war rather than let the nation survive; and the other would accept war rather than let it perish. And the war came.

One-eighth of the whole population were colored slaves, not distributed generally over the Union, but localized in the southern part of it. Those slaves constituted a peculiar and powerful interest. All knew that this interest was, somehow, the cause of the war."

Lincoln's view can of course, be dismissed as a simple statement of wartime propaganda, dressed up as a moral imperative. By 1865 the president had become the Great Emancipator, the one person who so firmly fixed the war in the popular imagination as a fight for freedom as well as for union.

By that time, the other president, Jefferson Davis, had changed his position as well. His initial justification for going to war was that it was necessary to protect the South's peculiar institution, but as the war progressed, he sought to raise it to a higher plane by citing the appeals of regional self-determination.

Other Confederate leaders were more blunt however, Thomas R. R. Cobb complained, "These hypocritical, fanatical miserable Yankees will not leave us alone to worship God and see our happiness as He has given us the right to do so. They invade our country. They burn our houses, ruin our property, steal our slaves and imprison our men and women and cruelly treat our children. What can we do but war with them?" Southerners argued that they were fighting to protect hearth and home and to restore respect for states' rights, rather than to keep millions in bondage.

Lincoln won the war, and it is clear Lincoln won the argument. But having said that, why did the war come after all? Why was the American Union disrupted? The role of slavery was, indeed, essential in precipitating the conflict, but the dynamics of its influence were rather complex. As Lincoln said, all knew somehow slavery was responsible – but how?

The Southern leaders in the 1850s often reminded the nation that the Constitution protected slavery and recognized the so-called peculiar institution in a variety of ways including special provisions for representation, taxation, and the slave trade. The most articulate statement of American liberty – the Declaration of Independence – was written on the leisure time of a planter who held two hundred slaves.

And the Founding Fathers purposely eliminated Jefferson's attack on the British king for promoting the slave trade. Later he concluded, "A geographical line coinciding with a marked principle, moral and political, once conceived and held up to the angry passions of men, will never be obliterated, and every new initiation will mark it deeper and deeper." Slavery was, he prophesied, "a fire bell in the night."

Thus, it is fair to conclude that the Union was conceived with slavery in mind, although the Founding Fathers and many others expected that slavery would eventually die out. Indeed, the critically important state of Virginia almost abolished slavery. Nat Turner's abortive slave revolt sent tremors throughout the South, but by the 1830s the cotton gin gave it a new economic lease on life.

I

The Southern apologists for slavery were correct in certain assertions. A good part of the world at that time permitted slavery, including their own nation. It was the North that dramatically changed in the period from 1790 to 1840. It was the North that began to see that slavery was not just a system of alternative labor, but a terrible moral dilemma.

Also, the plantation economy created a very different sort of ruling class in the South. Although the number of slave owners with large slave populations was limited, slave owners made up one-fourth of the South's populations. The "typical" slave owner owned five or six slaves; one-fourth of all slave owners owned 15 to 20 slaves; 10 percent of slave owners owned 100 or more.

But those numbers belie the real power structure of the old South. Historian Charles Sellers has concluded that this slave holding class had, "an aristocratic, anti-bourgeois spirit with values and mores emphasizing family and status, a strong code of honor, and aspirations to luxury, ease, and accomplishment."

By the 1830s and 1840s that new generation of Southern leaders was no longer embarrassed by slavery; they relished it, defended it, and sought its expansion. Jefferson and his contemporaries expected slavery to wither up, to lead to black immigration to Africa or Latin America, or somehow to be permanently ameliorated. Calhoun and his colleagues, however, boasted that race slavery provided the mudsill that all societies had to have in someway or another. These new apologists were aggressive in their defense, in ways that their fathers had once been apologetic.

Whereas Northerners in the past had accepted earlier those divisions of opinion, now they worried about different civilizations actually cropping up. William Seward pronounced the situation "an irrepressible conflict," and Abraham Lincoln warned about the inevitable collapse of a house divided against itself. The American people had strong ties – a common constitution, a common language, the same legal system, and a respect for the same heroes

– many of whom came from the South, especially from Virginia. They also had strong spiritual traditions based on Protestant religious beliefs, and there were substantial economic ties of course. Yet the war came.

In trying to explain that paradox, historian David Potter has argued persuasively that the South was very different – it was a folk culture with strong kinship ties, a hierarchical social system, specifically delineated statuses, patterns of deference, codes of chivalry and honor. The North was more urban, more industrial, more committed to economic change. In 1790 fewer than one in ten people lived in towns or cities; by 1840 one out of three people in New England and the Atlantic states lived in cities and towns. The opposite held true below the Mason-Dixon Line. Indeed, from 1810 to 1860 the percentage of capital involved in manufacturing in the South actually declined from 31 percent to 16 percent. Agriculture remained king.

But the war was not caused by the ratio of agriculture to manufacturing in that section, it was caused by slavery. The presence of racial bondage established a ruling class that was defensive, paranoid, arrogant, and increasingly assertive. Its leaders insisted that not only must the North accept what the North had already accepted, but that slavery be trumpeted by all as a positive good, that Northerners must be willing to hunt down fugitive slaves and return them to their masters, and that slavery must be allowed to expand into the western territories.

In some areas of the South where slavery existed nominally as in the border states, the power of the ruling class was sometimes less and the ties of rural southern farmers to the Union stronger. The loyalists in those Border States and the strength of Union sentiment in the western counties of Virginia and in Missouri clearly showed the limits of the slavery-holding way of life. However, in other states such as South Carolina, whites of very different classes maintained racial solidarity in support of slavery and its way of life. This is not to say that those Southern unionists were abolitionists or committed advocates of equal rights; they were often as prejudiced as those on plantations and those in urban areas in the North.

However, what especially troubled Southern apologists was the North's attitude of moral superiority. Southerners insisted that slavery was not just an unfortunate expediency imbedded in their economy; they maintained that it was a positive good and grew furious when politicians sought to contain it.

The Mexican War and the vast lands that President Polk claimed after it were seen in the North as part of a larger conspiracy to extend slavery past the older coastal states, into the hinterlands and beyond including into Cuba where the soil was more beneficial to plantation life than in the New Mexico territory.

Southerners believed at first that an alliance with the West would curtail the North's influence, but the opposite happened. The West with its restless young men and determined pioneer women became more entrepreneurial and less tradition bound. Those settlers appreciated Henry Clay's vision more than John C Calhoun's. The South did not sympathize with the West's demand for standing armies on the frontier or appreciate the need for internal improvements and greater infrastructure. By the beginning of the Civil War, the South provided two-thirds of the world's cotton crop, with three-fourths of that crop going to Great Britain. At times then it seemed that the master class looked east across the oceans rather than west across the mountains. It is no coincidence either that the new Republican party looked twice in 1856 and in 1869 to men of the frontier, John C. Frémont and Abraham Lincoln.

II

Southerners complained that it was not they who had changed, but the North. They still accepted the Union as it was once presented, with its rural lifestyle, states' rights, limited republican institutions, and a constitution that acknowledged human bondage as a legitimate way of labor. There is some truth to that argument. The North was changing economically, of course, but it was changing in other ways, ways that directly related to how people perceived the institution of slavery.

In the 1830s and 1840s, a series of reform movements which embraced every cause from abolitionism to free love, women's rights, temperance, education and prison reform, and even vegetarianism swept through the North. Foremost in the reform movement was the influence of New England which had been exporting for several generations large numbers of white people into adjacent areas, most importantly, the upper Midwest. The attitudes of New Englanders with their fervent religious sentiments, personal thrift, determined perseverance, and general seriousness were constantly remarked upon by observers of the time.

During this period those men and women were especially bound to evangelical Christianity. Religion infused their view of life and impacted on their thinking. Between 1800 and 1860 the combined numbers of Methodists, Baptists, and Presbyterians increased enormously. Those three denominations embraced over 80 percent of all church affiliated Protestants. Even away from local organized congregations, the ever presence of the Bible in homes and preacher-led renewals, revivals and tent meetings reinforced the importance of enthusiastic faith in Protestant life.

Some of those reformers may have used religion to compensate for the loss of political influence after the demise of the New England-based Federalist

Party or for their loss of the eschatological faith. But the passionate ways of reformers created a climate of self-criticism and deep moral scrutiny that somehow existed side-by-side with rugged individualism and acquisitive capitalism. It may be that such individualism made people especially prone to feelings of inadequacy, and that a preoccupation with worldly goods led people to seek more out of life. Thus, secular reforms gave meaning to one's life and informed one's daily activities.

In any case, the North and the West, to a lesser extent, were swept up in broad humanitarian and democratic reforms. And as that occurred how could any honest scrutiny not focus on slavery – that most terrible betrayal of the human spirit? Slavery denied a sense of progress which was so important to democratic peoples. It made a mockery of the promise of a more civilized way of life. Southern apologists tried to equate slavery with Sir Walter Scott's novels and their charming portraits of the idyllic, ordered feudal life, but there was too much of the lash in the slave order, too much breeding and selling of the black young, too much random violence and sexual exploitation. Slaves were not serfs, and the presence of race as a dividing line gave bondage a different and even more immoral definition. It was the image of Simon Legree, and not Ivanhoe that so fixed the popular imagination.

III

One can see that religious influence in the rhetoric of Abraham Lincoln. He was generally not considered an orthodox Protestant; indeed early in Lincoln's career, a local minister charged that he was an atheist or at least an agnostic, a characterization he denied. But in the searing furnaces of war, he insisted on appropriating the harsh God of the Old Testament as an arbitrator in the conflict. The best example is the God of Lincoln's second inaugural:

It may seem strange that any men should dare to ask a just God's assistance in wringing their bread from the sweat of other men's faces; but let us judge not that we be not judged. The prayers of both could not be answered; that of neither has been answered fully. The Almighty has His own purposes. "Woe unto the world because of offenses! For it must needs be that offenses cometh; but woe to the man by whom the offense cometh!" If we shall suppose that American Slavery is one of these offenses which, in the providence of God, must needs come, but which, having continued throughout His appointed time He now wills to remove, and that He gives to both North and South, this terrible war, as the woe due to those by whom the offenses came, shall we discern therein any departure from those divine attributes which the believers in a Living God always ascribe to Him? Fondly do we hope – fervently do we pray – that this mighty scourge of war may speedily pass away. Yet, if God wills that it continue, until all the wealth piled up the bondsmen's two hundred and fifty years of unrequited toil shall be sunk, and until every drop of blood drawn with the lash shall be paid by another drawn with the sword, as was said three thousand years ago, so still it must be said, "The judgments of the Lord, are true and righteous altogether."

The president had reached deep into the well of Protestant if not Calvinist allegories and found his Maker and Judge. Lincoln had a fine ear for public opinion and his cadences were more than simply stylistic. He used that theology of retribution to frame the great conflict and thus made himself and it immortal. Even on their finest days, Davis, Calhoun, Clay, and a hundred Sunday School preachers in the South could never explain the war in terms that a God-fearing people could fully appreciate.

Low tariffs, free land, and states rights did not give the South the moral plane that the abolition of slavery did. It is standard twentieth century historical scholarship to maintain that Southerners – the slave holding master class especially – did not know or accept the immorality of their peculiar institution. They felt no qualms – no guilt about human bondage, about mating slaves to produce children for sale and export, about resorting to violence and punishment on the plantation. It is hard to believe that all of that moral myopia was so. For one of the great critical edges that Lincoln had was emancipation – he raised a war for political union to a higher moral scale, and by doing so provided the North with a cause which even some of his adherents did not fully appreciate at first. Later even Jefferson Davis promised freedom to Southern slaves who fought for the Confederacy. But few came forward. There was to be only one Great Emancipator in this war.

Lincoln ultimately gave the sordid details of war a nobility to satisfy the terrible sacrifices in a way that Jefferson Davis was never able to do. Surely that judgment is somewhat retrospective, but it is clear that Lincoln's image as the Great Emancipator had some important appeal beyond the abolitionists who distrusted him and the slaves who had only vaguely heard of him.

Before the war, many Northerners had already claimed the moral high ground – as they insisted that slavery be contained in its current boundaries. They insisted on no expansion. It was on this question that the Republican Party was founded, Lincoln was elected, and the war began. The South recognized that a Republican president meant the end of the expansion of slavery in the new lands. What was at stake was not just the desire of free white men to own lands in the West and Southwest, but the moral implication behind the ban on black bondage in those areas, even though a good portion of the Southwest was not amenable to plantation or agricultural slavery.

Like the United States' proclamation of containment in the post-World War II world against the communists, the declaration of non-expansion of slavery carried a clear set of moral judgments about protecting oneself from the spread of contagion. The free-men/ free-land ideology may have solidified the Republican Party's appeal, but the South understood very well the language of moral condemnation.

When the Supreme Court in the Dred Scott case made slavery a national institution, the North began to see another conspiracy as well – one to extend the power and influence of Southern life everywhere, regardless of the local law or public sentiment.

Some historians have stressed the importance of economics, of Know-Nothingism, of religion or ethnicity in the coming of the war. But slavery was the necessary condition that made the war happen. Slavery created separate civilizations, broke up the common national organizations from churches to political parties, and created on both sides passionate minorities devoted to making slavery a great national issue. Republican politician Carl Schurz observed that slavery was "not a mere occasional quarrel between two sections of the country, divided by geographic link" but a "great struggle between two antagonistic systems of social organization."

And it is ironic that slavery led to the war that destroyed in a very short time human bondage in the United States which had existed without peril for nearly two centuries. Lincoln could barely hold the Union together without black troops in the armies, nearly 200,000 of them, and without raising the war to a high moral plane, thus keeping Britain neutral. Yet it was Ulysses S Grant, not Lincoln, who saw very early in the war that it would lead inevitably to an end to slavery. Slavery was the cause of the war, was the underpinnings of the Southern aristocracy's wealth, and was the prop that must come crushing down if the Union were to be one again.

CHAPTER TEN

SUMMARY REPORT OF U.S. DOJ INFORMATION ON EMPLOYMENT LITIGATION, HOUSING AND CIVIL ENFORCEMENT, VOTING, AND SPECIAL LITIGATION SECTIONS' ENFORCEMENT EFFORTS FROM FISCAL YEARS 2001 THROUGH 2007

By
U.S. Government Accounting Office

The Hall Institute of Public Policy has included a brief summary and some excerpts of the 180 page report done by the Government Accounting Office and the Department of Justice on civil rights enforcement efforts during the administration of President George W. Bush. The full report can be found on the U.S. GAO website at http://www.gao.gov/products/GAO-10-75. It is a rather critical report, and thus is an important historical treatment on employment litigation, housing and civil enforcement, voting and special litigation. The footnotes are the original report numbers and are unchanged here

Summary

The Civil Rights Division (Division) of the Department of Justice (DOJ) is the primary federal entity charged with enforcing federal statutes prohibiting discrimination on the basis of race, sex, disability, religion, and national origin. GAO was asked to review the Division's enforcement efforts. This report addresses the activities the Division undertook from fiscal years 2001 through 2007 to implement its enforcement responsibilities through four of its sections (1) Employment Litigation, (2) Housing and Civil Enforcement, (3) Voting, and (4) Special Litigation. To conduct our review, GAO analyzed data on cases filed in court and matters (e.g., a referral or allegation of discrimination) investigated. To supplement this analysis, GAO also reviewed a sample of closed matter files (about 210 of 5,400). GAO randomly selected matters investigated under different statutes for each section and considered the government role (e.g., plaintiff or defendant) and type of issues investigated (e.g., the nature of the alleged discrimination or violation) to ensure that the sample reflected the breadth of the work and practices of each section. While not representative of all closed matters, the sample results provided examples of why matters were closed. Additionally, GAO analyzed complaints and other relevant court documents for a comparable number of cases filed as plaintiff by each section, as well as DOJ documents, such as annual reports, that described the Division's enforcement efforts.

From fiscal years 2001 through 2007, the Employment Litigation Section initiated more than 3,200 matters and filed 60 cases as plaintiff under federal statutes prohibiting employment discrimination. About 90 percent of the matters initiated (2,846 of 3,212) and more than half of the cases filed (33 of 60) involved individual claims of discrimination. Of these cases, more than half (18 of 33) alleged sex discrimination against women. The Section filed 11 pattern or practice cases--cases that attempt to show that the defendant systematically engaged in discriminatory activities. Nine of these cases involved claims of discrimination in hiring, and the most common protected class (i.e., class of individuals entitled to statutory protection against discrimination, such as national origin or gender) was race (7 of 11). From fiscal years 2001 through 2007, the Housing and Civil Enforcement Section initiated 947 matters and participated in 277 cases under federal statutes prohibiting discrimination in housing, credit transactions, and certain places of public accommodation (e.g., hotels). Nearly 90 percent (456 of 517) of the Fair Housing Act (FHA) matters were initiated under its pattern or practice authority. The largest number of the FHA matters involved allegations of discrimination based on race (228) or disability (206). The majority (250 of 269) of the cases that the Section filed as plaintiff included a claim under the FHA and primarily involving rental issues (146 of 250). Most of the cases alleged discrimination on the basis of disability (115) or race (70). From fiscal years 2001 through 2007, the Voting Section initiated 442 matters and filed 56 cases to enforce federal statutes that protect the voting rights of racial and language minorities, disabled and illiterate persons, and overseas and military personnel and addressed such issues as discriminatory voter registration practices. The Section initiated most matters (367 of 442) and filed a majority of cases (39 of 56) as plaintiff under the Voting Rights Act. These matters (246 of 367) and cases (30 of 39) were primarily filed on behalf of language minority groups. The Section spent about 52 percent of its time on reviews of proposed changes in voting procedures (e.g., moving a polling place) submitted by certain jurisdictions covered under the act, as compared with cases (about 33 percent) or matters (about 14 percent). From fiscal years 2001 through 2007, the Special Litigation Section initiated 693 matters and filed 31 cases as plaintiff to enforce federal civil rights statutes in four areas--institutional conditions (e.g., protecting persons in nursing homes or jails), conduct of law enforcement agencies (e.g., police misconduct), access to reproductive health facilities and places of worship, and the exercise of religious freedom of institutionalized persons. Of the matters initiated and closed (544 of 693), the largest numbers involved institutional conditions (373) and conduct of law enforcement agencies (129). The cases filed (27 of 31) primarily involved institutional conditions. DOJ provided technical comments, which GAO incorporated as appropriate.

Why GAO Did This Study

The Civil Rights Division (Division) of the Department of Justice (DOJ) is the primary federal entity charged with enforcing federal statutes prohibiting discrimination on the basis of race, sex, disability, religion, and national origin. GAO was asked to review the Division's enforcement efforts. This report addresses the activities the Division undertook from fiscal years 2001 through 2007 to implement its enforcement responsibilities through four of its sections (1) Employment Litigation, (2) Housing and Civil Enforcement, (3) Voting, and (4) Special Litigation. To conduct our review, GAO analyzed data on cases filed in court and matters (e.g., a referral or allegation of discrimination) investigated. To supplement this analysis, GAO also reviewed a sample of closed matter files (about 210 of 5,400). GAO randomly selected matters investigated under different statutes for each section and considered the government role (e.g., plaintiff or defendant) and type of issues investigated (e.g., the nature of the alleged discrimination or violation) to ensure that the sample reflected the breadth of the work and practices of each section. While not representative of all closed matters, the sample results provided examples of why matters were closed. Additionally, GAO analyzed complaints and other relevant court documents for a comparable number of cases filed as plaintiff by each section, as well as DOJ documents, such as annual reports, that described the Division's enforcement efforts.

What GAO Found

From fiscal years 2001 through 2007, the Employment Litigation Section initiated more than 3,200 matters and filed 60 cases as plaintiff under federal statutes prohibiting employment discrimination. About 90 percent of the matters initiated (2,846 of 3,212) and more than half of the cases filed (33 of 60) involved individual claims of discrimination. Of these cases, more than half (18 of 33) alleged sex discrimination against women. The Section filed 11 pattern or practice cases—cases that attempt to show that the defendant systematically engaged in discriminatory activities. Nine of these cases involved claims of discrimination in hiring, and the most common protected class (i.e., class of individuals entitled to statutory protection against discrimination, such as national origin or gender) was race (7 of 11).

From fiscal years 2001 through 2007, the Housing and Civil Enforcement Section initiated 947 matters and participated in 277 cases under federal statutes prohibiting discrimination in housing, credit transactions, and certain places of public accommodation (e.g., hotels). Nearly 90 percent (456 of 517) of the Fair Housing Act (FHA) matters were initiated under its pattern or practice authority. The largest number of the FHA matters involved allegations of discrimination based on race (228) or disability (206). The majority (250 of 269) of the cases that the Section filed as plaintiff included a claim under the FHA and primarily involving rental issues (146 of 250). Most of the cases alleged discrimination on the basis of disability (115) or race (70).

From fiscal years 2001 through 2007, the Voting Section initiated 442 matters and filed 56 cases to enforce federal statutes that protect the voting rights of racial and language minorities, disabled and illiterate persons, and overseas and military personnel and addressed such issues as discriminatory voter registration practices. The Section initiated most matters (367 of 442) and filed a majority of cases (39 of 56) as plaintiff under the Voting Rights Act. These matters (246 of 367) and cases (30 of 39) were primarily filed on behalf of language minority groups. The Section spent about 52 percent of its time on reviews of proposed changes in voting procedures (e.g., moving a polling place) submitted by certain jurisdictions covered under the act, as compared with cases (about 33 percent) or matters (about 14 percent).

From fiscal years 2001 through 2007, the Special Litigation Section initiated 693 matters and filed 31 cases as plaintiff to enforce federal civil rights statutes in four areas––institutional conditions (e.g., protecting persons in nursing homes or jails), conduct of law enforcement agencies (e.g., police misconduct), access to reproductive health facilities and places of worship, and the exercise of religious freedom of institutionalized persons. Of the matters initiated and closed (544 of 693), the largest numbers involved institutional conditions (373) and conduct of law enforcement agencies (129). The cases filed (27 of 31) primarily involved institutional conditions.

DOJ provided technical comments, which GAO incorporated as appropriate.

Results-in-Brief

From fiscal years 2001 through 2007, the Employment Litigation Section initiated more than 3,200 matters and filed 60 cases as plaintiff under federal statutes prohibiting discrimination in employment based on race, color, sex, religion, national origin, and military service, and retaliation against a person for filing a charge of discrimination, participating in an investigation, or opposing discriminatory practices. About 90 percent of the more than 3,200 matters the Section initiated (2,846 of 3,212) alleged violations of section 706 of Title VII of the Civil Rights Act, which involve individual claims of discrimination. Additionally, about 96 percent of the matters (3,087 of 3,212) initiated were as a result of section 706 referrals from the EEOC and USERRA referrals from the Department of Labor.[78] As such, much of the Section's matters are driven by what the Section receives from other agencies. Consequently, the number of section 706 and USERRA matters initiated declined in the latter fiscal years, which Section officials attributed to a decline in referrals from EEOC and the Department of Labor, respectively. Because the Section did not require staff to maintain information in ICM on the subjects of the matters, such as harassment and retaliation, or the protected class, such as race and religion, of the individuals who were allegedly discriminated against, we could not determine this information for over 80 percent of the matters the Section closed from fiscal years 2001 through 2007. In our September 2009 report on ICM, we recommended that the Division require the sections to record data on protected class and subject in the

---

78 The Employment Litigation Section considers all EEOC charge referrals and Department of Labor USERRA referrals as matters even if an investigation is not opened. However, the section does not consider requests for right-to-sue letters as matters. While a charging party is required to file a charge of discrimination with the EEOC, according to Section officials, some charging parties may prefer to initiate litigation on their own and, in such instances, will request that DOJ provide a right-to-sue letter as obtaining a right-to-sue letter is a precondition to filing a Title VII claim in federal court. According to Employment Litigation Section officials, the section honors such requests and issued 14,608 such letters from fiscal years 2001 through 2007. (App. II includes information on the number of right-to-sue letters issued each fiscal year by the Section.)

Division's case management system in order to strengthen its ability to account for its enforcement efforts.[79] DOJ concurred with our recommendation. In addition to the matters initiated, the Section filed 60 cases in court as plaintiff from fiscal years 2001 through 2007, and filed more than half (33 of 60) under section 706 of Title VII. According to Employment Litigation Section officials, the primary reason for pursuing a case was that the case had legal merit, i.e., the strength of evidence in the case. The majority of the Section's cases (18 of 33) involved sex discrimination against women, and one-third (11 of 33) involved claims of race discrimination,[80] with six cases filed on behalf of African Americans and five cases filed on behalf of whites. For example, in March 2005, the Section filed a lawsuit alleging that the city of Cairo, Illinois, discriminated against a female employee by sexually harassing her, denying her a promotion, and terminating her employment because she refused sexual advancements from her supervisors. Most of the 11 pattern or practice cases the Section filed during the 7-year period involved claims of discrimination in hiring (9 of 11) and the most common protected class was race (7 of 11), with four cases filed on behalf of African Americans, two on behalf of whites, and one on behalf of American Indians or Alaska Natives. For example, in January 2001, the Section filed a lawsuit alleging that the Delaware State Police Department was discriminating against African Americans in hiring for trooper positions.[81] Of the 16 USERRA cases the Section filed from fiscal year 2005—the year the Section began filing these cases—through 2007, more than half (10 of 16) alleged violations of reemployment rights and/or discharge under USERRA.

From fiscal years 2001 through 2007, the Housing and Civil Enforcement Section initiated 947 matters and participated in 277 cases under federal statutes prohibiting discrimination in housing, credit transactions, and in certain places of public accommodation (e.g., hotels).[82] The Section enforced provisions of the Fair Housing Act (FHA), the Equal Credit Opportunity Act (ECOA), and the land use provisions of the Religious Land Use and Institutionalized Persons Act (RLUIPA), among others. According to Section

---

79 GAO-09-938R - http://www.gao.gov/new.items/d09938r.pdf

80 Individual cases can involve multiple protected classes and subjects.

81 African American refers to the protected class "black or African American."

82 One of the cases the Housing and Civil Enforcement Section filed was as plaintiff intervenor against multiple defendants. When the Section entered into a consent decree with some of the defendants, it created an additional Department of Justice (DJ) number–– a unique identification number assigned by DOJ when a matter or case is first entered into ICM––so it could track both the settlement and the remaining ongoing litigation; however, the Section treats this as one case, as there was one complaint.

officials, the Section considers legal merit when deciding whether to pursue a matter as a case as well as (1) whether it looks like the matter will be resolved locally, (2) whether litigation would resolve a significant statutory issue, and (3) whether the plaintiff has the resources to proceed on its own should the Section choose not to get involved. During the 7-year period, the Section initiated more matters (517 of 947) and participated in more cases (257 of 277) involving discrimination under the FHA than any other statute or type of matter or case. More than half (517 of 947) of the matters initiated involved an allegation under the FHA,[83] primarily alleging discrimination on the basis of race or disability and involving land use/zoning/local government or rental issues.[84] For example, the Section investigated a matter in which a landlord of an apartment complex allegedly turned away families with children or assigned them to a particular floor. According to Section officials, the large number of land use/zoning/local government matters it initiated was due to the Section regularly receiving referrals from HUD as well as complaints from other entities involving these issues. Over the 7-year period, the Section experienced a general decline of election matters involving an allegation under the FHA derived from HUD referrals, with the fewest number of total matters, 106, in fiscal year 2007. Section officials attributed the decrease, in part, to a decline in referrals from HUD as a result of more complaints of housing discrimination being handled by state and local fair housing agencies instead of HUD. The majority (250 of 269) of cases that the Section filed in court as plaintiff involved a claim under the FHA—more than half (132 of 250) of which involved a pattern or practice of discrimination. Additionally, more than half (146 of 250) of the FHA cases involved rental issues and nearly half (115 of 250) were brought on behalf of persons with a disability. For example, one of the complaints we reviewed was filed on behalf of a man with a disability who had filed a complaint with HUD against the property manager and owner of his apartment complex, alleging the defendants discriminated against him on the basis of his physical impairments when they unreasonably prolonged meeting his request for a ground floor apartment and did not provide the reasonable accommodation of an accessible parking space. The number of cases filed by the Section generally decreased from fiscal years 2001 through 2007 from 53 to 35, which Section officials generally attributed to fewer election cases being referred from HUD. Overall, almost 70 percent (185 of 277) of the cases the Section participated in from fiscal years 2001

---

83 This includes FHA either solely or in combination with ECOA and RLUIPA.
84 Rental matters involve discrimination in property that is listed for a fee, and can involve issues such as eviction, the discriminatory provision of services and facilities occupancy restrictions, and the assessment of rental fees based on the number of occupants.

through 2007 originally derived from a HUD referral, but declined to about 50 percent (17 of 35) of cases filed in fiscal year 2007.

From fiscal years 2001 through 2007, the Voting Section initiated 442 matters and filed 56 cases as plaintiff to enforce federal statutes that protect the voting rights of racial and language minorities, disabled and illiterate persons, and overseas and military personnel and address such issues as discriminatory voter registration practices. It enforced the VRA, the NVRA, UOCAVA, and beginning in fiscal year 2002, HAVA. The Voting Section has the discretion to initiate a matter or pursue a case under all of its statutes, with the exception of the review of changes in voting practices or procedures, which it is statutorily required to conduct under section 5 of the VRA. During the 7-year period, the Section initiated more matters (367 of 442) and filed more cases (39 of 56) under the VRA than the other statutes it enforced. The Section initiated most matters (246 of 367) on behalf of language minority groups, primarily Spanish speakers (203 of 246). For example, in one matter, the Section obtained copies of bilingual general election materials from the elections administrator to determine whether the jurisdiction was complying with requirements that it provide written materials and other assistance for elections (e.g., ballots) in the language of the applicable minority group. The Section also initiated 162 matters under section 2 of the VRA, which prohibits voting practices or procedures that discriminate on the basis of race, color, or membership in a language minority group. About half of these matters were initiated on behalf of language minority groups (80 of 162), primarily Spanish speakers (71 of 80) and about half involved a racial minority (88 of 162), primarily African American voters (71 of 88).[85] For example, one matter involved allegations that African American students at a college and a university faced discriminatory treatment in the registration process for the 2000 presidential election. The majority of the cases that the Section filed in court under the VRA were on behalf of language minority groups (30 of 39 cases), primarily Spanish speakers (27). While cases involving language minority groups were filed under various VRA provisions, the largest number of cases (24 of 30) involved claims under section 203 alleging that the covered jurisdiction had failed to provide voting-related materials or information relating to the electoral process in the language of the applicable minority group. For example, in one case, the Section alleged that, in conducting elections, a city, where over 46 percent of the total citizen voting age population was Hispanic, had not translated fully into Spanish written election-day materials and information, such as the official ballot, forms for voters with disabilities, and signs identifying a polling place's location, among others. The Section filed 13 cases that involved a claim

85 Seven matters involved both a language minority and a racial minority group and in one matter the specific protected class was not identified.

under section 2 of the VRA, 5 on behalf of language minority groups and 10 on behalf of racial minority groups—6 on behalf of Hispanics and 3 on behalf of African Americans.[86] For example, the Section alleged that certain voting practices—such as hostile acts direat Hispanic voters or requiring Hispanic voters to prove their citizenshiwithout credible evidence calling into question their citizenship—were in violation of section 2. According to aggregate data on time spent on matters, cases, and other activities for the 7-year period, the Voting Section reported devoting the greatest total percentage of time (52 percent) to administrative reviews of proposed changes in the voting practices and procedures of certain jurisdictions covered under section 5 of the VRA, such as a proposed redistricting plan––which would make changes to the geographic boundaries of voting districts––or the relocation of a polling place, as compared with cases (33 percent) or matters (14 percent).

From fiscal years 2001 through 2007, the Special Litigation Section initiated 693 matters and participated in 33 cases enforcing federal civil rights statutes in four areas––institutional conditions, the conduct of law enforcement agencies, access to reproductive health facilities and places of worship, and the exercise of religious freedom of institutionalized persons. The Section enforced the Civil Rights of Institutionalized Persons Act (CRIPA), Violent Crime Control and Law Enforcement Act (14141), Freedom of Access to Clinic Entrances Act (FACE), and the provisions of the Religious Land Use and Institutionalized Persons Act (RLUIPA) protecting the rights of free exercise of religion for institutionalized persons. The Section could bring cases involving the exercise of religious freedom under RLUIPA and access to reproductive health facilities under FACE, on behalf of individuals. However, the Section was statutorily required to file only cases that alleged a pattern or practice involving institutional conditions under CRIPA and 14141 and of police misconduct under 14141. Because the Section had discretion under all these statutes to pursue an investigation or case, it considered all of its work to be self-initiated. During the 7-year period, the Section initiated 693 matters and participated in 33 cases under federal statutes corresponding to its four areas of responsibility, but these matters and cases primarily involved institutional conditions. Of the 693 matters initiated, the Section concluded or closed 544 matters. The majority of the closed matters (373 of 544) concerned a wide range of allegations about institutional conditions in various types of facilities––adult corrections (e.g., jails and prisons), health and social welfare (e.g., nursing homes, mental health facilities, facilities for persons with developmental disabilities, and group foster homes), and juvenile corrections (juvenile correctional facilities or entire juvenile correctional systems). The allegations included failure to provide adequate medical, mental health, and

86 Two cases involved both racial and language minority groups.

nursing care services to residents; staff's physical abuse of residents; and overcrowding in the facility. The Section also initiated and closed 129 matters involving the conduct of law enforcement agencies, specifically allegations of police misconduct in law enforcement agencies, such as police use of excessive force (i.e., more than necessary to subdue a citizen). During the 7-year period, the Section participated in 33 cases—31 as plaintiff, 1 as defendant, and 1 as defendant intervenor. The majority (27 of 31) of the cases that the Section filed as plaintiff alleged a pattern or practice of egregious and flagrant conditions that deprived persons institutionalized in health and social welfare (13), juvenile corrections (7), and adult corrections (7) facilities of their constitutional or federal statutory rights. Cases involving juvenile correctional facilities constituted the largest number (7) of any one type of facility and included such allegations as a pattern or practice of failing to protect inmates from undue risk of suicide and abuse from staff; failure to provide adequate mental health, special education, rehabilitation therapy, or psychiatric services; use of isolation or physical restraints; and failure to provide the number of professional staff legally required for that type of facility. According to Special Litigation Section officials, the Section filed two of the seven cases because the respective jurisdiction refused to cooperate with the Section and settle the case. The Section filed the other cases because Section officials believed conditions in the juvenile facilities were so egregious that filing a case was the proper avenue for the Section to monitor the respective jurisdictions' remedial efforts. In addition, the Section brought cases against two city and one county police department. All three cases alleged police use of excessive force. According to aggregate data on the time spent on matters and cases from fiscal years 2001 through 2007, the Section reported devoting the greatest percentage of time (62 percent) to matters and cases (81 percent) involving institutional conditions, as compared with its other areas of responsibility.